PEOPLE ARE BIGGER THAN THE PROBLEMS THEY FACE

People Are Bigger Than The Problems They Face
Copyright © 2018 Ira L. Lake, PhD., M.Div., M.A.

Imtasik Family Counseling Services Inc.
Riverside, California
5101 Seri Court
Riverside, CA 92509

Book design by:
Arbor Services, Inc.
www.arborservices.co/

Printed in the United States of America

People Are Bigger Than The Problems They Face
Ira L. Lake, PhD., M.Div., M.A.

1. Title 2. Author 3. Self-Help

Library of Congress Control Number: 2017914781
ISBN 13: 978-0-692-95685-4

PEOPLE ARE BIGGER THAN THE PROBLEMS THEY FACE

Ira Lake, PhD., M.Div., M.A.

Imtasik Family Counseling Services Inc.

Dedication

To the only wise God be glory and majesty, dominion, and power forever Amen. If it were not for God where would I be? So, I thank my God for all that he continues to do on my behalf and for giving me the opportunity through this book to positively impact lives. I also want to thank my wonderful wife Sara for your constant encouragement and support and for believing in my dreams.

My father Richard C. Lake was the biggest influence in my life and I dedicate this book to him. It was because of you Dad that I learned my work ethic and drive to excel. For all you sacrificed so that I could have every advantage and opportunity to be where I am today I thank you. you are my hero and role model. To my stepmother Elaine Lake thank you for being so kind and gentle. You entered my life and helped nurture me. Dawn (my stepsister). I thank you for your support in all things.

To my three daughters Taylor, Loryssa, and Torrie you ladies are my inspiration and I want you to know how proud I am of each of you. I love and treasure you dearly.

Sharon Jones and Sandy Ballinger (my play moms). I would not have made it this far if it had not been for your kindness and encouragement.

And to my (play Sister) Michelle Buckman, I often think of the times you helped me construct sentences and understand concepts when I was working on my doctorate. Thank you so very much.

This book is also dedicated to the many couples and singles who are in and/or would like to be in a healthy relationship. The tools provided in this book combined with your desire will help you create and sustain a healthy relationship

Contents

Chapter 1
The Five Key Essentials

When a relationship ends, people often ask themselves, "What went wrong?" While it's natural to wonder, this question is often the wrong one to ask. "What went wrong?" starts with the assumption that the relationship began as healthy and stable and then something happened to change it. In my experience, many relationships are threatened by problems that exist long before the two people even meet one another. In fact, many of us carry problems with us that prevent relationships from even starting. So when I talk about repairing damaged relationships, I'm often speaking to men and women who aren't even in a relationship yet. Think of it as preventive maintenance, like brushing your teeth every day so that you don't have to see a specialist to handle that cavity.

Of course, before we can explore what threatens a healthy relationship, it's a good idea to establish what constitutes a healthy relationship. How do you know a relationship is healthy? Is it a relationship without fights? Is it a relationship with constant sex? Is it a relationship in which each person is "getting what they want" out of it? Those relationships can certainly appear to be strong . . . and yet we've seen such relationships fall apart, seemingly overnight and for no obvious reason.

Generally speaking, a relationship is considered healthy when each partner's needs are being fulfilled. What are those needs? With some variation, both men and women have four essential needs that they want fulfilled in a relationship. Women are generally looking for open communication, affection, intimacy (or emotional security), and strong spiritual leadership from a husband. Men are generally looking for domestic support, sex on a regular basis, respect, and fellowship with friends outside the home. Obviously, there is some overlap between genders. Furthermore, same-sex couples often split these needs in different ways between partners.

While the needs of each partner may be different, I've found five key essentials to maintaining any healthy relationship: learning to change your mindset, building trust, honest communication, true intimacy, and conflict resolution skills. If one or more of these key essentials are not in place, a relationship is certainly possible, but it won't be a healthy or stable one. Not only must these essentials be present for a solid, long-term relationship to be possible, but they need to be present for both partners. You can't have a relationship with one good communicator and one bad communicator, for example, or with one partner willing to change and the other unwilling to change.

Again, plenty of relationships can form where one or more of these key essentials are missing, but over time it will become apparent to the partners—if not to those around them—that something is missing. Sometimes, both partners recognize what's missing and find that fixing the problem on their own is possible. But more often, they require a third party (not a friend or family member who will take one or the other's "side") to speak with them and offer a fresh perspective. I've spoken with hundreds of couples and individuals about relationship troubles. While each person and couple is unique, patterns nevertheless emerge. What follows are a series of true stories that detail how one missing key essential can either damage a relationship or prevent one from even starting. I've included an example of both a couple and a single person to illustrate the need for each of the five key essentials. Since a vital aspect of my work is maintaining confidentiality, the names and other identifying information about these individuals have been changed.

Chapter 2
Changing Your Mindset

Quite simply, your "mindset" is a collection of the opinions and perceptions about the world around you. For most of us, our basic mindset is set quite early in life, usually before we have begun a formal education in school. In fact, by the age of three, our mindsets are already well established. This isn't to say that we maintain the mind of a three-year-old throughout our adult lives, but we do carry many strong opinions from that age. This can be the age when prejudices and phobias are first formed, both of which constitute irrational opinions that no doubt make perfect sense to a three-year-old. It can also be the age when we develop our ideas about what constitutes a healthy relationship. It is one of the reasons why so many children of abusive parents, abused parents, and negligent parents grow up to be abusive, abused, or negligent themselves.

This isn't to say that a mindset formed at the age of three can't be changed later in life. Significant events such as the death of a loved one, abuse, or divorce can certainly still have an effect on our emotional growth past age three. On the other hand, as we mature, we are also capable of consciously changing our mindsets. Of course, the first obstacle to making such a change arises when we can't tell the difference between what's real and what we perceive to be real. If you believe that all relationships have to be abusive, then you won't necessarily see nonabusive relationships, but simply relationships where the abuse is well hidden. If you believe that all relationships are doomed to failure, then you will simply dismiss stable relationships as the ones that will fall apart in the future. The human mind is remarkable in its ability to filter out information that disagrees with a preformed set of ideas, focusing only on those things that reinforce what it already believes. So if those preexisting beliefs are toxic, the person who holds them will continue to hold them, even when evidence proves those beliefs are wrong and even when those beliefs are shown to harm the individual.

A faulty mindset can make it difficult to see how you're sabotaging a relationship because of unrealistic expectations or unfounded fears. Even beginning a relationship is difficult if you always expect them to end badly. Furthermore, you may receive no indication from the people around you that anything is wrong, since to all appearances, you're a perfectly decent person who can't seem to make a relationship work for some reason. Maybe you'll even be told that you're just "unlucky in love," when luck has nothing to do with it.

William and Cynthia
One of the false assumptions that so many people make about failed relationships is that one partner or the other is responsible for "messing it up." What I've discovered, time and again, is that both partners will,

more often than not, contribute to a relationship's failure. In fact, many times one of the things these partners end up having in common is whatever fractured worldview eventually threatens the relationship.

To an outside observer, William and Cynthia seemed like an ideal couple. Both of them were successful in their chosen professions; William was a computer analyst and Cynthia a certified public accountant. Both of them were shy and introverted. Neither of them stood out in a crowd. Neither wanted children. And neither was ever seen arguing with the other. As far as mindsets go, an outside observer might assume that they had similar—and therefore compatible—views of the world.

In fact, many of their similarities provided clues to the problem that threatened to end their marriage. Both William and Cynthia were afraid of being hurt in a relationship. This fear extended to more than just their marriage, and the reason they were both so shy in any public situation was due to a fear of developing any sort of close relationship, including friendships. Since they were both so experienced at keeping their feelings hidden, they rarely had any arguments because neither of them offered anything for the other to argue about.

The reason neither of them wanted children was because a child would simply make a divorce more difficult. Likewise, they kept separate bank accounts. When I spoke with them, each confessed to having an "exit strategy" already worked out for what they both perceived as their relationship's inevitable end. In fact, within six months of getting married, they were each preparing for a divorce.

Of course, what they considered to be an exit strategy, someone else might call a self-fulfilling prophecy.

But why should either of them believe that their relationship was doomed from the start? After all, neither of them was physically, verbally, emotionally, sexually, or financially abusive toward the other. They respected one another and, in many ways, got along well with one another. They were friends. Why would a deeper relationship not be possible?

First of all, both William and Cynthia came from broken homes. William's parents got a divorce when he was twelve years old, after his mother found out about an affair that his father was having. Cynthia's parents divorced when she was nine years old. In addition to dealing with her parents' divorce, Cynthia also lost most contact with her father, who wasn't active in her life (save for the child support checks that he regularly sent to her mother). And while Cynthia's mother dated several men after the divorce, none of those relationships lasted for more than a year.

For both William and Cynthia, the divorces occurred after their third birthdays. So both of them already had a mindset in place in regards to what made a strong relationship. In both cases, a new event managed to change their mindsets. While the changes were negative, we should take hope from the fact that their mindsets were changed, which if nothing else shows that mindsets can be changed as we get older. The problem now was to figure out a way to once again change their mindsets, this time in a more positive manner.

Of course, the first step in dealing with any problem is to recognize that a problem exists. Between separate bank accounts and a lack of children, William and Cynthia easily ignored their problems altogether. Their mutual dedication to their careers made it even easier, as they both spent a lot of time at the office, and away from one another. The little time they did spend together was pleasant but guarded. They were always careful to keep those emotional walls in place, and while that prevented arguments, it also prevented true intimacy.

So if they were both planning to leave, if they were both convinced that their relationship was doomed, why bother seeking help? Quite simply, they wanted more than separate lives alone. They also wanted more than a pleasant but cold relationship. They wanted a genuine loving relationship. I truly believe that everyone wants that sort of relationship, one that provides attachment, security, and love. William and Cynthia had so much in common, and they realized that they also shared this longing. The reason they hadn't previously created such a relationship on their own was that their fear had been stronger than their longing, but now they were ready to face that fear.

When I say "fear," I think it's important to remember the source of most fear is the unknown. We fear an uncertain future or a confusing present. For both William and Cynthia, divorce was a known quantity, and while unpleasant, they were both confident that they could live with it. But trust and intimacy . . . they'd never seen those work in a relationship (again, keep in mind that their mindsets often made them filter out the healthy relationships that were all around them, focusing only on the negative). If each of them opened up to the other, truly trusted another person, they didn't know what would happen. When I use the term "exit strategy" to describe their plans for divorce, I don't do it lightly; "exit strategy" is the same term used by abused spouses who are planning to escape their abusers. This couple was using the same strategies to avoid one another that men and women who are physically abused use to save their lives. That's fear.

How to help them change their mindsets? I began with some basic cognitive behavior therapy methods. Learning to change how you perceive a situation in order to change your actions is more or less the definition of cognitive behavior therapy. So rather than beginning with a list of things they were doing wrong, I asked them what they imagined to be a typical relationship. I then explored where they got these ideas about relationships. Of course, many of their ideas came from their own divorced parents, but a lot of them also came from television. These days, many of our ideas originate from television, which is an imperfect reflection of reality, to say the least. Television by its nature needs to maintain high drama in order to keep people's attention, which means that it mostly shows couples that are constantly arguing, breaking up, getting back together, cheating on one another, and basically doing everything in their power to not build stable foundations.

Obviously, a couple of divorces and hundreds of make-believe relationships are not a strong foundation to build on, so I followed up by asking William and Cynthia to list their basic goals and dreams. Specifically, I wanted them to list their personal goals and dreams, not ideas about an ideal relationship. Only after they'd made their lists did I ask them to compare those lists against each other. Of course, they were surprised to find that many of their goals and dreams were identical. This was the foundation that a relationship could be built on. Once they had this foundation, I next had to help them accept that neither a "perfect" marriage nor a "one-size-fits-all" marriage existed. By changing their mindset to view marriage as a partnership rather than a test they would inevitably fail, they were able to open up to one another, trust one another, and communicate better with one another.

After only two sessions together, the couple saw improvement. By the end of five sessions, I felt I had done everything I could for them. They began keeping journals to better express their thoughts—to themselves and each other—and promised to get in touch with me every few months to let me know how they were doing. And while I'd love to say that this sort of progress is typical, the fact is that counseling will often take far longer and involve far more obstacles. After all, William and Cynthia weren't cheating on one another, and no abuse was involved. I've used them as an example to show that even a relationship with no obvious problems can be missing some key essential.

Marshall

While relationships can suffer if one or both partners have a toxic mindset, the fact is that far more people never get into a relationship in the first place because of toxic mindsets. Not only do these distorted values make building trust and intimacy difficult, but no one is present who can point them out. Even if William and Cynthia had trouble recognizing their own mistaken worldviews, they could recognize one another's mistaken worldviews and point them out to each other. People like Marshall, on the other hand, never got close enough to anyone for a long enough period of time to have such shortcomings pointed out. The end result is often an attitude that everyone else in the world "has a problem."

Like William and Cynthia, Marshall came from a broken home. His mother and father divorced when he was only thirteen years old. While he maintained a close relationship with his father, he developed an emotional distance from his mother. Over time, he came to blame his mother completely for the breakup and, on a certain level, began to distrust women in general.

As Marshall grew older, he developed a roundabout method of avoiding long-term relationships, while at the same time pretending that he wasn't distrustful of women. In fact, he dated frequently and was even involved in a number of relationships. However, all of these relationships were extremely short lived (never lasting for more than a year at most and usually for a far shorter amount of time). Marshall never directly ended these relationships himself; rather, the women would always leave him. In this way, he could convince himself that he was making an honest effort to reach out to women and that they simply weren't worth his time or trust . . . reinforcing the mindset he'd developed as a teenager. But what Marshall wasn't admitting to himself was that he was manipulating the women in his life in various passive-aggressive ways so they would decide to leave him without even realizing that this was what he wanted them to do. Again, no one was close enough to Marshall to point out that he was doing this.

As with Cynthia and William, Marshall sought to change because, despite his mindset, he truly did want to form some sort of lasting relationship. Eventually, he sought out counseling. Initially, the counseling was based around the question of "Why do I keep dating the wrong sort of woman?" Since they always left him, of course it would stand to reason that it was their fault that the relationships had ended. We've all heard the question: "Where are all of the good women?" A similar question is asked equally often: "Where are all of the good men?"

The answer, of course, is that the world is full of good women. Not only that, but Marshall had already been in relationships with a number of them. Because the problem wasn't that he was looking for a "good" woman, but rather that he was looking for a "perfect" woman. And when each of the women he was dating failed to live up to that standard, he would drive her away, without leaving her outright.

By the time our first counseling session was over, I'd already seen the problem with Marshall's mindset. Marshall believed that his mother had left his father (and Marshall) because she was flawed in some way. Therefore, he would try to find a woman without any flaws, believing that such a woman could therefore be trusted to always do the right thing. Of course, in his case, doing the "right thing" meant staying in a relationship with him.

It's totally natural to focus on an ex-partner's flaws after a relationship has ended, especially if he or she is the one who left you. Some of it is a "sour grapes" style of thinking. "Oh, she wasn't so great anyway." "I'm better off without him." "She was just holding me back in my career." "He was a loser." And when I asked Marshall about his ex-girlfriends, I got many of the same comforting observations. One of his ex-girlfriends had been too heavy. Another one was too aggressive. Still another one didn't share his religious beliefs. He always had a reason why he was better off without them. And since they were the ones who always left him, he could rationalize that it was never his fault that the relationships ended.

But the truth was that Marshall didn't want to "settle" for a woman who was less than perfect. So when he decided that whichever woman he was dating at the moment was flawed in some way, he'd begin to withdraw from her emotionally. He'd nitpick at her flaws and spend less time with her. He developed a passive-aggressive personality so he never had to do any direct confrontation. Rather, he would let the women feel increasingly uncomfortable until they ended the relationships for him, thus keeping him safe from commitment, while at the same time leaving him feeling completely innocent of any responsibility for ending the relationship himself.

Besides his relationship trouble, Marshall was also looking for help dealing with issues of low self-esteem and lack of confidence. Of course, these issues were directly tied in with his relationship troubles. In a way, Marshall blamed himself for his parents' divorce; this is quite common. While his unrealistic expectations for a partner might seem grounded in arrogance (thinking that nobody was "good enough" for him), the truth was that he felt that only a "perfect" woman would be able to stay in a relationship with him. And when each of the women he dated eventually left, his self-esteem plummeted even further, meaning that the next woman had an even higher hurdle to clear in order to be considered perfect enough for him. The first step in his treatment, therefore, was to come to terms with his parents' divorce and stop blaming himself for it.

Building up Marshall's self-esteem was a twofold process. First, I pointed out that he had a number of good qualities, such as being intelligent and well spoken. Of course, a good example of his intelligence was the masterful way that he'd manipulated so many women to leave him without ever giving away that they were doing exactly what he secretly wanted (in effect, being so clever that he outsmarted himself out of a relationship). So while I built up his self-esteem by pointing out his intelligence, I needed to build it up further by encouraging him to apply that intelligence to something more productive that alienating women.

I suggested that Marshall join a men's support group in order to better communicate his problems and fears. While regular meetings with a therapist can be a helpful first step in recovery, the therapist/ client relationship is too isolated and controlled, with one person giving help and the other person receiving help. In a group setting, things are less predictable and closer to "real life" situations. Furthermore, no one is simply passively receiving help, but also actively giving help to people with similar problems. Since he obviously had problems speaking openly and honestly with women, joining a men's group (as opposed to a mixed-gender group) ensured better results.

The support group that Marshall joined was affiliated with a church but did not promote any religious worldview. The meetings were held in a church basement, and that was the extent of the group's connection to any religious institution. This worked well for Marshall, who'd never considered himself strongly religious (despite having complained that one of his ex-girlfriends wasn't a good match because they didn't share the same faith) and didn't feel alienated from any of the other members because of differing spiritual beliefs. That said, over time, Marshall became more heavily involved with the church and enjoyed the feeling of community that it provided. Again, when helping people with relationship problems, I'm dealing with more than just problems with romantic relationships. What Marshall needed was help in making any sort of emotional connection with other people, even casual friendships.

Once we made progress with Marshall's self-esteem issues, we could begin looking at his past relationships and why they ended. He eventually acknowledged that his behavior was passive-aggressive. He also acknowledged that his standards for an "ideal woman" were unrealistic. Of course, the first step in acknowledging that the standards were unrealistic was to get him to verbalize them. I asked him to describe aloud what he considered to be an ideal woman. Quite simply, he was looking for an independent career woman who also possessed cooking and domestic skills.

Now, a woman who is both a dedicated professional and a dedicated homemaker is going to be a tall order. In fact, it's almost a contradiction. If she spends too much time at work, then she's neglecting her domestic duties. If she spends too much time at home, then she's neglecting her career. Either way, she wouldn't be able to measure up to Marshall's standards, and he'd drive her away in his own subtle way.

Obviously, the next step in Marshall's counseling was to work on his unrealistic concept of a perfect woman. Instead of focusing on why the woman he was looking for couldn't possibly exist, I instead tried to get him to change his focus to his own goals and dreams rather than on a potential partner's qualities. What did he want to do with his life? What sort of partner would work well with those goals in mind? Because of Marshall's passive-aggressive tendencies, a woman who was more direct and assertive would be better suited for him than someone who wanted a quiet, domestic role. Generally speaking, a career-minded woman was going to be more independent and therefore more aggressive than someone more interested in a domestic role. And since he was spending so much time outside of a relationship anyway, it might be a good idea if he learned to cook and clean for himself.

Once Marshall began setting more realistic goals (looking for someone who would make a good life partner rather than someone who was perfect in every way), he realized that he'd already met a number of women who fulfilled these criteria. In fact, he'd dated a number of them and driven them away because of his heightened expectations. One of the sad truths of relationship counseling is that people won't appreciate the good relationships they had in the past until they're gone and beyond salvaging. However, this regret is tempered with the knowledge that they can make better decisions going forward.

After eight sessions, Marshall had achieved a new level of confidence and a more realistic set of expectations for relationships. We maintain contact and, while Marshall hasn't yet found a stable, long-term relationship, he is dating and confident that he will do a better job of nurturing a relationship in the future.

Action Steps

While I often recommend counseling for couples and individuals who need to change their mindsets, the simple fact is that there are things most of us can do on our own to help with this problem. If William and Cynthia's story or Marshall's story seems similar to your own life situation, you can take action right now to correct a faulty mindset.

One step you can take is role modeling. Quite simply, role modeling occurs when you seek out positive-minded people and try to mirror their behaviors and ideals. Obviously, I'm not advocating surrendering your individuality to be exactly like someone else. But chances are that you know at least one person with a situation similar to your own: a victim of abuse who nevertheless trusts his or her current partner, someone who's been cheated on multiple times yet continues to pursue new relationships (albeit cautiously), or someone who is supportive of a partner despite that partner's flaws. You could observe this individual and see how he or she deals with problems that normally overwhelm you. Or you could simply ask this person how they manage to stay so positive during times of stress. Again, joining a support group can be a wonderful way to find people with similar problems you could role model.

Another step you can take is to honestly examine your beliefs and then consider how those beliefs coincide with the reality of your life. While this can mean religious beliefs (and many people refuse to even consider dating someone outside of their faith), it can also mean simple nondenominational values. Do you want to raise children? Do you want to devote the bulk of your time to a career? Do you want a quiet life with a small group of friends, or a loud life with lots of friends and travel? While the old saying goes that "opposites attract," the fact is that you are going to need a lot of common values in order to build a life together with another person. The alternative is staying in a relationship built on endless compromise, where each partner believes that he or she is sacrificing more than the other and ends up resentful.

Both role modeling and examination of your beliefs requires a good deal of honesty (with yourself if no one else). And the problem with faulty mindsets is that they often make such personal honesty difficult, if not impossible. Therefore, seeking counseling or joining a support group are often necessary follow-ups after taking those initial action steps.

Chapter 3

Building Trust

The second key essential to maintaining a healthy relationship is the ability and willingness to build trust with another person. Obviously, most of us don't trust people instantly. At least, we don't completely trust anyone upon first meeting him or her. First dates are often exercises in determining how much each person can trust the other. Second dates are usually built on some basic initial trust, then expanding on it. Think about how long you had to know your husband or wife before you could trust them completely, and you'll probably realize the sad truth: you've never learned to trust them completely.

The fact is that most of us maintain a certain level of distrust throughout our relationships, and in many cases, a small level of distrust can be healthy. I want to stress that I'm talking about only a small level of distrust.

By contrast, the men and women coming to see me often have more than that healthy of level of distrust. This isn't simply a suspicion that he's cheating on you if he works late and comes home smelling like perfume. It's not the suspicion that she's socking some money from your joint account into a secret account of her own when the monthly balance doesn't add up. This is wondering what your wife is implying if she asks, "How was your day?" This is wondering if your husband is planning to leave you every time he's too exhausted to have sex. This is not telling your wife when you're worried about your job or not telling your husband when you're worried about a lump you found while you were in the shower. This is being afraid to share any bad news with your spouse or partner because you don't know how they'll handle it. This is being afraid that every day of your relationship is the last one, that the other person has been planning to leave you for months, that anything you say might be that breaking point, that it's better to say nothing and not take the chance that someone you love will react badly.

Relationships without trust often appear ideal from the outside looking in. After all, people who don't trust each other aren't honest with each other. And people who aren't honest with each other only share the good news, the bland parts of their lives, with one another. People who don't trust each other don't give each other anything to fight about.

But relationships without trust often fall apart as soon as there's trouble. When your first instinct is self-protection, truly supporting another person when they're having trouble is difficult, just as it's difficult to accept such support when you're in trouble yourself. Unfortunately, one of the few certainties in any relationship is that, sooner or later, there will be difficult times, so a relationship without strong trust will crumble, sooner or later.

I'll often refer to trust as the load-bearing wall of a relationship, since it's the wall that the other key essentials rest against in order to keep a relationship stable. Without trust, we can't take a chance on changing mindsets that (from our point of view) have kept us safe for years. Without trust, communication will only be about surface issues, lacking deeper understanding between partners. Without trust, true intimacy is impossible; sex can be present, but it will usually be quite shallow. Without trust, conflict resolution becomes impossible because we'll always be looking at such resolutions as changing ourselves or giving up something without the confidence that the other person will change or give up anything in response.

Of course, on the flip side of the trust issue is the fact that not everyone is truly worthy of trust. In fact, many people develop trust issues because they trusted someone in the past who betrayed them in some way. This goes back to the first key essential, changing your mindset, with the fact that acknowledging the need for trust isn't enough. We have to be willing to risk betrayal or abandonment in order to build trust with another person.

The fact is that nobody is going to be completely trustworthy in all ways. We all have our weak points, and sometimes we simply don't notice the situations in which trust is being placed in us. When your girlfriend asks you to meet with her at a certain time, you might blow it off as an unimportant coffee date, while she considers it a test to see if you can carry through on a simple promise. When your husband says he doesn't care if you meet your ex-boyfriend for a drink, he might be expressing a profound level of trust in you rather than indifference. We're all damaged in some way by past relationships (romantic and otherwise), and the amount of trust we're willing to place in someone will vary greatly between people.

I spend more time dealing with trust issues than with any of the other key essentials. And I've learned that no single method works for every couple to help build trust. That's because trust manifests itself in different ways for each couple, indeed for each individual. And like learning to change one's mindset, a lack of trust can both damage an existing relationship as well as an individual's ability to enter into a relationship in the first place.

Christopher and Karen

By this point, it might seem as if whether or not a relationship is stable can be determined by whether or not the parents of those involved got a divorce. And while divorce can be traumatic for the children of the couple getting the divorce, it doesn't follow that all children of divorced parents will have problems in their own adult relationships. In the same way, having a stable upbringing with happily married parents is no guarantee of a stable relationship in adulthood. Christopher and Karen provide an excellent example of a couple coming from two quite different backgrounds, yet developing many of the same problems in regards to trust.

Christopher's parents divorced when he was young. Nothing was obviously "wrong" with the relationship; there was no physical, sexual, or verbal abuse between his parents. Quite simply, his parents simply drifted apart. Like a lot of men in a single-income household, his father would often work long hours and assume that his financial support of the family was a sufficient level of commitment. But his mother needed more than simply a good provider in her life and, rather than verbalizing this need (with or without seeing a therapist), she chose instead to leave him. Again, we have a relationship in which neither partner is solely to blame, since neither of them communicated openly with the other, yet also a relationship in which each partner is able to place the bulk of the blame on the other (he was never around, she never said there was a problem). And since Christopher's parents never communicated these problems with one another, they certainly never communicated them with their son, leaving him to form his own fractured mindset.

Christopher grew up watching his mother go from one boyfriend to another, never developing a strong relationship with any of them; I won't try to guess what sort of relationship issues she was working through. After the divorce, Christopher's father ceased to be an active part of his life; again, I was never told whether his father remarried or otherwise worked through whatever problems he'd had in the relationship. So Christopher grew up without an idea of how a stable relationship worked, as well as without any sort of stable male role models. As he matured, he began entering into relationships of his own, but these relationships were always short lived (similar to the ones his mother was in) and almost always based on nothing more than sex.

Karen, on the other hand, grew up in a stable household. Her parents were happily married, and she recalled no major troubles in her childhood. She felt secure and had strong role models, both male and female.

I mentioned earlier the concept of a healthy level of distrust, especially early in relationships. Due to her ideal upbringing, Karen was ironically unable to spot warning signs that the men she chose as boyfriends were untrustworthy. She would enter into these relationships with far too much trust and openness, giving new boyfriends far more benefit of the doubt than they'd earned or, as it turned out, deserved.

Karen worked as a nurse, a stable job with a decent salary. Her early boyfriends would often take advantage of her, using her for money. They would also lie to her and cheat on her. In fact, she told me that, before she'd met Christopher, every single one of her previous boyfriends had cheated on her. One of her ex-boyfriends had a drinking problem and would frequently lose jobs because of it, consistently turning to her for financial support while he failed to deal with his problems. Since Karen prided herself on being a trusting person, she would routinely forgive these men, giving them second chances (and third and fourth chances) that they didn't deserve. In the long term, this trust led to more than just financial losses, but also a loss of self-esteem.

Eventually, there is only so much trust and forgiveness that any one person can hand out before seeing it as pointless. Sure enough, Karen eventually became cynical about relationships in general, shifting from an initial attitude of complete trust to one of complete distrust. Obviously, neither of these extremes would serve her well in maintaining a stable, long-term relationship.

Of course, this distorted mindset gave her something in common with Christopher. Like Karen, Christopher never entered into relationships with a sense of trust, but rather kept his guard up. The only major difference between them was that Christopher had learned to distrust people at a far earlier age than Karen.

Again and again, the desire among damaged people to avoid relationships is overpowered by their need for intimacy. Despite what both Karen and Christopher had been through, they still wanted to form some sort of connection with another person, which is why both of them joined a dating website, where they eventually met one another. Unlike Karen's previous boyfriends, Christopher had a stable job (he was a high school history teacher) and no substance abuse problems. Unlike Christopher's mother, Karen seemed to be interested in maintaining a stable relationship with one person. On a surface level, each of them seemed to be the sort of partner the other one wanted.

As with other damaged relationships, everything seemed fine to outside observers, as Christopher and Karen didn't fight, didn't cheat on each other, and appeared to be exactly what the other wanted. But the damage done by previous relationships was profound, and they found that they couldn't connect on the sort of deep, emotional level that other couples connected on. They had contentment but lacked intimacy.

To their mutual credit, Christopher and Karen both realized that something was missing from their relationship, even if nothing seemed to be "wrong" with it. So they sought counseling.

While they both had problems with trust, the origins of those problems were quite different. I thought it best if I met with each of them individually before bringing them both into a couple's counseling session. After two sessions with Karen and two with Christopher, I had a fairly solid idea of where each of them was coming from, as well as an idea of what each wanted and expected from a relationship (keeping in mind that "want" and "expect" are often different).

The first step they needed to take to improve their relationship was to establish trust on minor issues. As stated earlier, we often create trust tests in the form of minor commitments. In their case, it was something as simple as Christopher saying, "I'll be back in a couple of hours," and actually being back within a couple of hours. Often those humble beginnings train us to trust people in much larger ways. Since both of them had suffered from a betrayal, part of establishing trust was confirming this common bond. Quite simply, neither of them wanted to be a betrayer in their current relationship, so they had to trust that the other person felt the same way.

Another trust exercise they engaged in was exchanging secrets with one another. This took place outside of my office (since they didn't have to share these secrets with anyone but one another). Quite simply, they'd lie in bed, beneath the covers, and share something secret about themselves. I don't know what they specifically shared with one another, but in many ways the specific secrets aren't important; the trust and intimacy of the sharing would increase their trust in one another. And, over time, Karen and Christopher did learn to trust both each other and other people.

I should be fully honest about this relationship and say that, eventually, Christopher and Karen did break up anyway. Sometimes the damage done in a relationship prior to counseling is simply too extensive to be repaired. Other times, the couple simply has compatibility issues that no amount of counseling resolves. About one out of every four couples that comes to me for counseling eventually breaks up.

In Karen and Christopher's case, they found it simply too easy to revert back to old habits of reservation and fear. While I believe they honestly approached the exercises with the best of intentions, those old habits were simply too ingrained in their natures.

However, this isn't to say that Christopher and Karen didn't benefit from counseling. I believe that the trust exercises they went through will help them to form stronger relationships with other people in the future. Shortly after the breakup, Christopher reached out to me with an interest in continuing his sessions on a one-on-one basis; as of this writing, he hasn't followed up on this initial interest. Karen also reached out for private counseling, and we continue to work together on her trust issues.

Judy

Until now, I've defined childhood trauma largely in terms of how stable the parents' relationships have been. But the fact is that children can suffer other, far more damaging, types of trauma than the divorce of their parents.

When Judy was thirteen years old, she was sexually abused by her paternal grandfather. In and of itself, this is traumatic, but the damage was compounded when she tried to tell her mother what had happened. At first, her mother told her that it wasn't true and accused her of lying. Such an accusation can also be traumatic. But things became even worse when Judy realized that not only did her mother already know about the abuse, but everyone in her family was aware of it as well. So at the age of thirteen, she had to cope with sexual abuse as well as the knowledge that her entire family would do nothing about it, in effect endorsing it with their inaction.

Eventually, Judy's abuser was arrested and sentenced to prison for what he did to her, but the sense of betrayal (by both him and the rest of her family) did significant damage to Judy's mindset that lasted well into adulthood. She had no self-confidence and never pursued an education past high school. At the age of thirty-eight, she was working at a retail job and almost never dated.

Of course, the reason most people seek out counseling is that they want to change some part of their lives. Judy wanted to go to college and get a better job. She also wanted to start dating and eventually get married. She knew that she couldn't develop self-confidence or a sense of trust on her own, so she sought professional help.

The reason for Judy's distrust of men in general made sense, given the betrayal of both her grandfather and the rest of her family. Many books have already been written on rape culture and how the inaction of others serves to further empower sexual abusers. Of course, it's often more than simple inaction, since Judy's mother actively defended the man who'd abused her, even though she knew that her daughter was telling the truth. Later in life, it was only logical for Judy to distrust men who outwardly seemed nonthreatening. Not only could they potentially be abusers, but if they did abuse her, Judy had no reason to think that anyone would help her (or even believe her). So in many ways, her trust issues weren't only with men, but with people in general.

Again, a certain level of distrust should be considered healthy in adults. Judy was not wrong to believe that some of the men she knew could be potential rapists. Sexual abuse is an epidemic around the world, and it sadly falls to women to take precautions to keep themselves safe from such abuse. It's also true that, in many cases of sexual assault, the victim is either disbelieved or outright blamed for the crime. For these reasons, I was not going to advocate that Judy be completely trusting in new relationships.

On the other hand, lifelong isolation from relationships was not a healthy option either. At the age of thirty-eight, Judy had already allowed a quarter-century of her life to be lost to childhood abuse. She needed to find some middle ground that would allow her to form emotional connections, while at the same time maintaining her personal safety.

During our initial meeting, I wasn't surprised to learn that Judy spent most of her time outside of work in her home. She rarely spent time anywhere else, she engaged in no activities that would put her in contact with new people, and she had no pursuits that would provide her with a sense of accomplishment. This fed both into her sense of isolation and diminished self-confidence.

The first step in her recovery process was learning how to dissociate her past from her present. What her grandfather did to her was wrong.

The way that her family (specifically her mother) had reacted to her abuse was wrong. Distrusting her grandfather and her family for what they did was understandable and justified. But extending that distrust to everyone she knew, to the point where she never risked a relationship, was doing more harm to herself than to the people she was shutting out of her life.

Of course, she required more than just intellectual exercises. Even though Judy accepted that not all men were rapists and not everyone was an enabler, that knowledge didn't help her to form new relationships. Acknowledging that you have a fear is not the same as facing it. So one of the simplest things that Judy had to do to deal with her isolation was to leave her home for some reason other than work or grocery shopping. Since she had no hobbies and wasn't enrolled in any classes, I suggested that she go to a shopping mall and sit in a food court. For the first few weeks of her counseling, she would spend between thirty and forty-five minutes a week sitting in a shopping mall and observing people. She didn't have to speak with them, didn't have to give anyone her phone number, and didn't have to place any social pressure on herself more than simply being physically present around strangers. In time, she did begin casual conversations with people who sat beside her. Who knows, perhaps some of the people she met were doing the exact same exercises.

Eventually, Judy joined a gym, which not only placed her near a large number of people, but also made her more active. Spending so much time alone in an apartment, watching television while barely moving around, can lead to serious health problems as well as social problems. As of this writing, she's already lost fifteen pounds. And while she didn't feel ready to date yet, it did help her self-esteem that several of the men at the gym had asked her out on dates.

Judy's gym membership led directly to a new interest in running. She joined a group that runs together once a week, providing both physical exercise and social interaction. Eventually, she began participating in a number of charity runs, which built further connections with her community.

Judy also joined the Kiwanis Club and began doing charity work knitting blankets for babies—as a part of their appropriately named "Blankets for Babies" program. While knitting can easily be a solitary activity, she opted to knit with a group of eight other women. While all of the women in her knitting circle are older than her, she's grown quite close with them.

As of this writing, Judy has enrolled in summer classes and is beginning the process of earning a college degree. After her shopping mall exercises, her gym membership, her knitting circle, and her participation in various running events, she was no longer intimidated by the social demands of attending classes. When I asked about her major, she told me that she planned on becoming a counselor, using the insights gained by her own traumatic experiences to help other people.

When we first met, Judy said that she'd chosen me specifically after reading my first book, Messed Up and Don't Even Know It. That book contained several accounts of childhood abuse that resonated with her. I hope that she will one day be able to use her own troubled childhood as a way to reach out to other people, rather than as an excuse to withdraw from them.

Action Steps

As with changing your mindset, chances are that many of the people reading about Judy or Karen and Christopher will see more than a little of themselves in these individuals. Maybe you use betrayals in previous relationships as an excuse to avoid trusting someone in your current relationship. Maybe this distrust extends beyond romantic relationships so you don't trust people in general and try to keep to yourself. And maybe you want to take steps to rekindle your ability to trust other people. On the other hand, perhaps you're in a relationship with someone who has difficulty trusting you and are looking for a way to help him or her open up.

One step you (and your partner) can take to build trust is to agree to always be honest with one another. Perhaps that seems obvious and perhaps you're thinking that you're already honest with your partner. But when your husband, wife, girlfriend, or boyfriend asks how your day went, how often do you say, "Fine," when it wasn't fine? How often do you agree with something that you believe is wrong simply to keep the peace? How often do you tell a "small lie" to avoid an argument? How often do you tell a lie so your partner won't worry about something that's bothering you? Too often, we think that trust simply involves trusting someone enough to believe they're not lying to us, but it also means trusting someone enough to share the bad parts of our lives as well as the good parts.

Another step we can take to build trust in our relationships is to say what we mean and mean what we say. That sounds nice, but what does it mean? How often do you choose words that are technically true but are bound to be misconstrued by your partner? "There's nobody I'd rather spend my life with than you," sounds nice, but it's not necessarily the same as saying, "I want to spend my life with you." "I want to have children" isn't the same as saying, "I want to raise children with you." "I have everything I want in my life" isn't the same as saying, "I'm happy with my life." Oftentimes, we're so clever that we trick ourselves into staying in a damaged relationship, always choosing statements that are technically true but not honest, to convince our partners and ourselves that everything is fine.

Of course, the most obvious step we can each take to ensure that our partners are reliable is to make sure that we're reliable ourselves. Be where you say you'll be when you say you'll be there. Follow through on promises and commitments. Never assume that our partners will understand if we break our word to them so that we can keep it to someone else. There are only so many times you can choose to honor commitments to friends or jobs over commitments to a spouse before that spouse rightly feels like a low priority. The simplest way to stay reliable is to never take your partner for granted.

Most of all, don't keep secrets from one another. As a counselor, I have to accept that there are things that my clients won't tell me. However, I'm still surprised at the trust many people will place in me that they don't place in their husbands, wives, boyfriends, and girlfriends. The more secrets you maintain from the people you love, the more you'll end up developing a second life, an existence separate from who you are when you're with them. The simple fact is that, if you tell enough lies to the person you love, you'll eventually lose track of the differences between your true self and the person you pretend to be. Keeping secrets not only speaks to a lack of trust but a lack of self-esteem, as it shows someone who believes his or her true self cannot be loved.

Chapter 4
Communication

First of all, communication involves a lot more than just talking. Chances are that the people you know who consider themselves to be the best communicators are, in reality, talkative people. And simply talking a lot doesn't necessarily make one a good communicator. You no doubt know some people who constantly complain about being misunderstood after talking at length about a topic. Sometimes the problem is that they provide so much unimportant information that the important stuff is lost in it all; such people have trouble "getting to the point." Sometimes a topic makes people so uncomfortable that they essentially "talk around" it, implying and suggesting without outright stating their opinions or concerns. They tell themselves that they had a "good talk," when in fact nobody else knows what they were trying to say.

And then, of course, some people talk but don't listen. These are the people who simply repeat their opinions over and over again without bothering to hear anyone else's ideas or point of view. Perhaps they believe that considering other points of view will make them appear weak. Or maybe they've simply held onto an idea for so long that they don't want to accept that they might have been wrong all that time. Or maybe they simply don't care enough about their partners to hear them out.

The reasons for poor communication skills—as with any other damaged key essential—can often be traced back to childhood. In many cases, the everyday environment is to blame rather than a specific traumatic event. Being told by a parent to "shut up" on one occasion probably won't leave much of a lasting impression. But being told to "shut up" on a daily basis for years will certainly reduce a child's sense of personal value. On the flip side, providing a completely permissive environment in which children are allowed to speak whenever they want, interrupting adults and other children, will likely result in a child with an overdeveloped sense of self-importance and an underdeveloped sense of other people's importance.

Good communication stems from both mindset and trust. Without a healthy mindset, communicating a problem is often impossible because one can't see that a problem exists or understand what the "real problem" is. Furthermore, men and women with damaged mindsets are more likely to misinterpret what other people tell them, in order to fit their preexisting notions. Trust is also essential for any sort of honest communication about sensitive topics; without trust, most of us will end up either saying whatever we think the other person wants to hear or reading secret meanings into whatever they tell us.

While each of us has our own method of communicating, I've noticed some distinct differences in how men and women communicate with one another. Men tend to speak on a surface level, often trying to "get to the point" and figure out the solution to a problem as quickly as possible. While this type of communication works well for simple, everyday situations, it's a poor method for dealing with more complicated issues. Women tend to speak on a deeper and more emotional level. While this type of communication is better suited for the subtle problems that can face a relationship, it's also not terribly clear and can be easily misinterpreted. As an example, if a couple were facing problems with intimacy, a man might oversimplify the problem in a rush to "solve" it, while a woman might talk a great deal about the matter without ever "finding the right words;" the result is that she thinks he's "not listening," while he thinks that she's "babbling."

When referring to problems of mindset or trust, couples often have to deal with identical issues, since both of them have a damaged worldview or difficulty trusting other people. When it comes to communication problems, however, couples often have polar opposite problems. One of them will talk too much, while the other one won't talk enough. One of them will listen so closely that they imagine hidden meanings in what they're told, while the other won't even hear surface comments. And despite the gender differences I mentioned earlier, it's not always the man who talks too little and the woman who talks too much. Sometimes men, especially successful men who are accustomed to not being questioned at work, will address their wives in the same tone as they address their employees, not bothering to listen to their input. Women who have suffered abuse—either in a current relationship or in previous ones—will often be reluctant to speak up on any issue, meekly going along in order to avoid conflict.

And of course a couple will suffer communication problems if both partners are too talkative or not talkative enough. You've no doubt met the obnoxious couple who not only talk over you, but also over one another. Neither of them hears what the other is saying, but both assume that they are being heard and understood. You've also met the couples who rarely speak at parties or with one another, blending into the background and never drawing attention to themselves. And you're probably surprised when you learn that such couples have broken up since "they seemed to have so much in common." A disregard for what other people have to say is not a strong common ground any more than a fear of being heard.

Without true communication—honestly speaking AND honestly listening—true intimacy will not be present in a relationship. For many people, an inability or unwillingness to communicate makes even starting a relationship impossible. When I counsel people who have trouble communicating with one another, I stress that both partners have to be willing to say things that might make the other person feel uncomfortable, while at the same time picking and choosing information so that they don't end up babbling about a lot of unrelated matters.

Lewis and Abigail

Lewis and Abigail were another example of a couple that, to the casual observer, seemed to be perfectly fine. They rarely argued. Neither was cheating on the other. There was no abuse. They had two healthy children and a nice house. Neither of them came from a broken or abusive household nor had a history of trauma. I'm sure that a lot of their friends would have been surprised to discover that they eventually sought counseling. Because as it turned out, Lewis and Abigail had several serious problems threatening their relationship.

While this couple certainly had troubles concerning mindset and trust, the primary problem was a lack of communication—more specifically, a lack of effective communication. Lewis was a naturally introverted person and generally didn't have much that he wanted to say. Abigail, by contrast, was open about expressing her feelings. Conversely, Lewis was good at listening to people, while Abigail lacked effective listening skills.

It's worth noting that Lewis and Abigail's situations influenced their behaviors. Lewis worked full time as an accountant, while Abigail was a stay-at-home mother raising their three-year-old and eighteen-month-old children. Lewis spent his days interacting with a variety of clients and coworkers, speaking on complicated subjects, so it made sense that at the end of the day he'd want to quietly relax at home. Abigail, on the other hand, spent her days with small children, so she had little in the way of mature conversation and by the end of her day was starved for interaction with adults.

So what could the two of them discuss? Not only would Lewis be tired of talking about accounting issues by the end of a busy day, but his wife would have almost nothing to contribute to such a conversation. So what they discussed most of the time were the children and what happened during Abigail's day. And while Lewis could certainly listen to what his wife had to say, he had little to offer as a response and, honestly, didn't much care what she was saying anyway. He did a lot of silent nodding, accompanied by the usual "uh huh" and "yeah" that would prompt her to continue talking.

Unfortunately, as anyone who's raised children will know, it's easy to become acclimated to a different way of talking (call it "baby brain" if you like). Abigail would sometimes listen to Lewis the same way that she would with a child: scanning for important key words, but otherwise ignoring most of it as nonsensical babble. How often do you seriously listen to what a five-year-old says and how often do you just nod through most of their nonsense? Now imagine conversing with an adult in the same way.

The one thing that Lewis and Abigail did have in common was their relationship with one another. At the end of the day, Lewis generally didn't want to talk about anything as deep as their emotional connection, while Abigail was so accustomed to speaking on the level of a three-year-old that she found it difficult to adjust the conversation to a more mature topic. They each showed their love for one another in other, nonverbal, ways. Lewis worked hard to provide for his family, while Abigail took care of the house and children while he was away.

But the problem with nonverbal communication is that many of us end up adding our own missing dialogue to it, imagining what the other person wants to say but might be afraid to. Abigail noticed that the two of them weren't as close to one another as other couples she knew and began to wonder if Lewis still loved her. Of course, she would bring up these concerns with Lewis, but he couldn't think of the proper words to respond—or he could think of them but wasn't certain that they were the proper words—and decided it was better to say nothing than risk saying the wrong thing. Abigail took this silence as confirmation that her husband no longer loved her. And when Abigail then stopped asking about her husband's feelings, Lewis would assume that his silence had been the proper response. So it was next to impossible to communicate the problem in their relationship because the problem was literally the inability to communicate with one another.

Fortunately, Abigail didn't want to give up on their relationship without trying to salvage it, so she sought out a counselor, which is how they met me. Lewis, of course, was reluctant to come at first since he didn't see the relationship as having any problems. On top of that, people who feel uncomfortable talking about their feelings will be reluctant to meet with a counselor for obvious reasons; getting people to talk about their feelings is pretty much what we do. I could tell that he was mostly there for the first few sessions because his wife wanted him there. Rather than voice his objection, he simply chose to silently go along with whatever she said. Sitting in on the counseling sessions, nodding along when Abigail and I were speaking . . . they were the basic nonconversation skills he'd been using for years. Ironically, the indifference that threatened their marriage was the same indifference that got him to attend counseling sessions in the first place.

After our first session together, it was obvious that Abigail was talking too much and not listening enough, while Lewis was listening too much and not talking enough. I imagine that Abigail was a bit surprised that part of the problem in the relationship was with her behavior as much as her husband's. Oftentimes couples will come to me trying to figure out who is at fault in a relationship; they may not say so out loud, but that's often at the heart of what they want to know. And oftentimes, both partners are at fault in one way or another. This is especially true in matters concerning communication skills, where neither participant can act solely as a listener or as a speaker.

Of course, Lewis loved his wife, but while he showed it in a variety of ways, he rarely said it. And while Abigail was desperate for her husband to try reaching out to her emotionally, she didn't realize that her constant talking made him feel uncomfortable "interrupting" her in order to offer his own opinions. So they both had some issues to work on.

Furthermore, they both had to accept that not every conversation they shared needed to be a deep meditation on their love. Their relationship needed lots of empty, casual conversation between them as well. But by making an effort to have those deep conversations once in a while, the casual conversations wouldn't feel so loaded with subtle clues about what they were truly feeling.

For example, if all you did was talk about the weather, the person you were speaking with would begin to suspect that talk of clouds, winds, heat, and cold were intended as metaphors for something else that you didn't feel comfortable discussing. "He was complaining about the weather a lot today; I wonder what's really bothering him." But if you openly talked about those deeper issues as well, then a conversation about the weather could just be a conversation about the weather. So the first thing I asked Lewis and Abigail to do in order to create more casual conversations was to set aside time once or twice a week when they would have those deeper conversations, what a lot of people would call "pillow talk".

While setting aside special times to talk is one positive step, the fact is that both of them were very busy throughout the week and often didn't have much time to communicate their deeper feelings on a regular basis. My solution for this problem was for the two of them to begin keeping a "love journal." Lewis would write something that he loved about his wife every morning before he went to work. By the end of the day, Abigail would have written something that she loved about Lewis in response. This way, the two of them each received a daily affirmation of love from the other one, even when they didn't have the time or energy to engage in any deep conversation face-to-face. At the same time, a love journal forced each of them to devote at least a little time every day to thinking about one another, reducing the risk that one would ever take the other for granted.

Of course, damaged relationships are rarely repaired with a "quick fix" solution, so they continue to see me twice a month. But their communication skills and relationship are already stronger for the effort that each of them has put in.

Deborah

I've said before that neglect is a form of abuse and that it can damage our spirits in ways similar to physical or sexual abuse. Unfortunately, unlike those other, more explicit, types of abuse, neglect often goes unnoticed. Quite frankly, it's right there in the name; if you're not paying attention to someone, then you probably won't be paying attention to the harm you're doing to them. This is why even the people closest to Deborah probably wouldn't have understood the problems she was going through.

Again, like so many of the other people who eventually came to me for help, Deborah's life probably seemed fine from the outside looking in. She had a stable job, no health problems, and a seemingly stable marriage. Her husband was even-tempered and well-respected within their community. And if she seemed to be a bit too quiet, that probably didn't seem like a cause for concern. After all, lots of happy people are quiet. There was certainly no reason to suspect that her husband was abusing her, either physically or sexually. In fact, it might be more accurate to state that Deborah was abusing herself, reinforcing self-destructive habits that she'd developed as a child.

Deborah was raised in a stable household. Her parents were married. She was never physically or sexually abused. She had no physical disabilities. Her family was financially stable, so there was no stress concerning money or embarrassment about having less than her friends. To the casual observer, she grew up as a child with no problems.

Unfortunately, Deborah was never a particularly assertive child. Again, there was no significant cause for her introversion; some children are naturally extroverted and assertive while others aren't. And as we can all remember, children are quick to interpret introversion as weakness and equally quick to take weakness as an excuse for bullying. True, the bullying was mostly teasing and taunting rather than physical beating, but words can render a tremendous amount of damage on a low self-esteem, and Deborah could still remember what those children said to her decades later.

As is all too often the case in these situations, Deborah didn't tell anyone about the bullying she endured. An element of shame keeps most people silent, a cultural expectation that they should be able to stand up to such bullies on their own without having to ask for help from others. While that was certainly how Deborah felt, she also had the problem of being emotionally distant from both of her parents. While they weren't divorced and still lived in the same house with her, neither of them was present—physically or emotionally—most of the time. Her father was a salesman who was on the road quite a lot. Her mother was an administrator for a school district, a job that kept her away almost as much as her husband. Deborah had no siblings, so she would often spend a great deal of time alone in her home.

When infants or young children are left alone, we rightly condemn these actions as neglect. But once children reach an age when they can prepare their own meals and know enough not to talk with strangers, we tend to think that they're fine on their own. And while spending some time alone can teach a child important life skills such as self-reliance, consistently leaving them on their own can deprive them of equally vital social skills. Quite simply, if a child learns how to live alone, then that is likely the sort of life that she or he will end up pursuing, while a child who learns how to coexist with others—both asking for help from and providing help to others—will probably pursue a more social existence.

Between the bullying at school and the neglect at home, Deborah became more introverted as she grew older. On top of that, she never developed the self-esteem necessary to pursue a fulfilling career. Eventually, she found work as an administrative assistant and settled into that career. As far as I could tell, she had no strong interests or hobbies that she pursued outside of her job. Her life was neither bad nor good, neither soul-crushing nor spiritually fulfilling. It was comfortable and safe, but that was all.

While she'd never dated much, Deborah did eventually marry. She met her husband, Kendrick, at her church. In fact, Kendrick was a church leader and extremely extroverted. As with Lewis and Abigail, they were in a relationship where one partner was far more talkative than the other. And while Deborah might have been glad at first that her husband was essentially holding up the social end of their relationship, it didn't help her to cope with her personal problems. She might have been going out to more social events with Kendrick, but she wasn't becoming more social.

Over time, both Deborah and Kendrick realized that their relationship had issues. Despite the absence of any abuse, she was always afraid to speak up or make her opinions known. They lived together, never fought, and would go out together, but Deborah never felt a strong emotional connection with her husband, and he didn't feel a strong emotional connection with her either. Kendrick was worried that the problem was with him, that he was somehow intimidating her. Of course, Deborah wasn't able to effectively communicate the problem because her problem was that she had poor communication skills.

Eventually, Deborah suggested that counseling might be a good idea. Kendrick agreed and was supportive during her first few sessions. I don't want this fact to go unappreciated. In many situations where a spouse has trouble communicating, counseling can be seen as a sort of betrayal. The logic might go: "You can't talk to me, but you can talk to this stranger." Despite the problem being tied up in Deborah's past, Kendrick might have understandably taken the introduction of a third party to be an invasion of his privacy, but he chose to be supportive of her decision.

Again, not only was Kendrick supportive, but after the first three sessions, he began to attend sessions with her as well. Let me be clear that he began attending after being invited by Deborah and me. This was not a situation where he insisted on getting involved.

Once the two of them were attending counseling sessions together, we began working on a series of directed exercises to increase her confidence and communication skills. In fact, they both developed better communication skills, which began with learning to listen effectively (i.e. listening to understand rather than just waiting for your turn to talk). These exercises continued weekly for a month and a half before Deborah was finally able to speak with confidence, and her husband was able to listen in an encouraging way.

One of the simplest exercises I had them both try was for one to repeat back what the other was saying in his or her own words. Not only did this confirm that each was being understood by the other, but it also served to validate what they were saying. Deborah was assured that she was being heard and that what she had to say had value. This exercise also had the added value of revealing to each of them that sometimes what they were trying to say and what the other person understood were different.

I also encouraged them both to focus on using positive terms. For example, Kendrick might ask Deborah, "Why won't you open up to me?" But a better statement might be, "I think you have something to tell me and I want to hear it."

Despite their success in improving their communication skills, Deborah and Kendrick still come to see me once every month or two. After all, effective communication isn't the sort of skill that can be mastered in a matter of weeks, and there's always more to learn.

Action Steps

One of the biggest obstacles to improving communication skills is that people often confuse "talking" with "communicating." Therefore, many of the worst communicators believe that they're the best communicators; they don't keep themselves open to input from their partners and don't even check to make certain that they're being understood or listened to. This is why most of the activities I suggest to improve communication skills break down to learning to listen better.

First of all, you need to make sure that you listen to understand rather than listen to respond. How can you tell whether or not you're doing this? After you finish an important conversation—whether with a spouse, friend, or coworker—you could take a minute to jot down two lists. On the first list, write down all of the key points that you mentioned in the conversation. On the second list, write down all of the key points that the other person mentioned. You might be surprised to find that the first list is much longer than the second and that you have trouble remembering what exactly the other person said. Be aware, while someone is speaking, what it is that you're thinking about. Are you looking for answers to questions or are you rehearsing what you're going to say in response?

Another key to effective listening is paying attention to more than the words being spoken. Does the person speaking with you look relaxed? Are his or her arms crossed against their chest, indicating that they are closed off from listening? Is the speaker's expression neutral, a sign that they might be trying to conceal their true feelings? Does the person take long pauses when they speak, as if what they're saying is emotionally difficult to reveal or they're unsure of what they're trying to communicate? And when you're speaking, does the other person remain focused on your face or does he or she frequently stare off in other directions? It's a fairly safe bet that anyone checking his or her phone while you're speaking isn't listening to you.

Of course, when you're speaking, it's important to be honest. While this is true in most conversations, it's especially vital when communicating with a loved one. When we're speaking with coworkers or casual acquaintances, it's common to tell small lies or omit minor details. Consider a question such as "How are you doing?" When your coworker asks that question, you'll likely say "fine" because the details of what's bothering you are not his or her concern. On the other hand, when a spouse or other loved one asks, hiding concerns over health, finances, or other personal matters creates a distance between you. Previously, I've mentioned how otherwise extroverted individuals often have trouble communicating with their life partners, and one of the reasons is because the social skills that work so well with crowds and business associates are often disastrous when trying to communicate with those closest to you. Don't be afraid to look weak, flawed, or wrong with the people who love you.

I mentioned earlier that saying what you mean and meaning what you say is important when communicating. Again, this isn't the same as telling the truth and not keeping secrets. We all learn ways to choose our words so that what we say is technically true while at the same time easy to misconstrue. For many of us, communicating with a partner becomes a sort of game in which we address all of the required topics while minimizing the emotional reactions of other people. Bad news from a doctor is minimized to being "probably nothing, but they want to run more tests." A fear of being fired becomes a concern over "being left out of the loop." A suspicion that your partner is abusing drugs becomes a question of whether or not he or she is "feeling all right," "getting enough sleep," or "stressed about something." While you don't want to hurt someone with your words, total honesty means risking some short-term pain in order to provide (or receive) long-term help. So when you're choosing how to break important news to a partner, try putting yourself in their place and ask yourself two questions: "If I were hearing this, what would I think was being said?" and "When I learned the truth, how would I feel?"

Of course, it's all too common for people to verbally attack one another under the guise of "just being honest." What begins as honest communication about honest concerns can devolve into petty name-calling. That's why, when you're trying to honestly communicate with your partner, you also need to maintain focus on what you're discussing. If you're concerned that your wife is drinking too much, there is no point in bringing up her weight or poor decisions she's made in the past or how her family treats you. If you're concerned that your husband might be developing a gambling addiction, bringing up the job he lost or criticizing his sexual performance isn't relevant. Yes, the two of you may have more than one problem to discuss, but each should be handled at different times; otherwise, your partner will be left with the impression that you're "dumping" a bunch of complaints all at once.

One way to prevent that "dumping" is to bring up concerns as you have them, rather than letting them fester for weeks, months, or years. If you don't maintain a steady line of honest communication, if you let your concerns "build up," then you're at a far greater risk to blurt out everything at once, overwhelming your partner and preventing any chance of constructively addressing any one of the issues that concern you.

Effective communication is in many ways a sort of balancing act: not withholding information, not giving out too much information at once, not staying silent to spare someone's feelings, not being needlessly cruel when speaking, and paying attention to nonverbal cues. But like any other skill, it becomes easier with practice.

Chapter 5

Intimacy

Inevitably, when I mention "intimacy," many people think that I'm talking about sex. And while reduced intimacy can lead to sexual problems (as reduced sexual activity can lead to intimacy issues), sex and intimacy are two very different things. In fact, many of the couples I see that have intimacy issues don't report having any sort of sexual problems.

So what is intimacy? Quite simply, intimacy is emotional honesty. You feel safe with another person and that person feels safe with you. The usual "barriers" that we put up when we're at the office, meeting with casual acquaintances, or interacting with strangers are brought down for one particular individual.

And how do we establish intimacy? We can start by maintaining the first three pillars of a healthy relationship that we've already covered: changing our mindsets, learning to trust, and developing communication skills.

For most of us, intimacy is learned when we're children. Our closest emotional bonds are often with our parents and siblings for the simple reason that they are our first and oldest bonds. Our relationships with immediate family members are often the things that teach us how relationships work. That's why toxic or nonexistent family relationships can end up teaching us toxic mindsets that impair our ability to form stable relationships later in life. So a part of building intimacy involves changing those mindsets when necessary.

Of course, emotional honesty implies a certain level of emotional vulnerability. Opening up emotionally to another person does involve the real potential for betrayal. And if you've learned not to trust other people as a coping mechanism after previous betrayals, that opening up becomes impossible, which makes intimacy impossible. So another part of building intimacy involves building and maintaining trust with another person.

Of course, even if you're willing to change your mindset and to trust another person with your emotional well-being, you might not know how to communicate your feelings with that other person. While we can learn communication skills from our immediate family growing up, keep in mind that those closest to us have learned to understand us even when we don't communicate effectively. Think about how often your parents or siblings have said something that might sound offensive or cruel if you didn't interpret what they "meant to say." So another part of building intimacy is learning to communicate properly, both in expressing your emotions to others and understanding that communication is more than simply the words being spoken.

Another factor to consider when building intimacy is gender. Whether the cause is genetic or the result of cultural training, men and women tend to have different ideas of what constitutes intimacy. While this isn't always completely true for all couples, both partners in any relationship must understand that they are often saying different things when they say there's an "intimacy problem."

With men, intimacy often translates as sexual openness. A "problem with intimacy" is often viewed as code for sexual dysfunction, which becomes a problem when I ask about intimacy issues and the husband immediately denies having any. The problem is compounded when a female partner suggests that the couple has an intimacy problem, which is then misinterpreted as a criticism of his sexual performance or an accusation of impotence. Of course, many men do have problems with sexual dysfunction, and this can then lead to an emotional distancing from their partners. On the other hand, a lack of emotional connection can eventually lead to a loss of sexual desire. Sexual performance is not the same as intimacy, but poor sexual performance can be either a cause or effect of diminished intimacy. Furthermore, men can often see a lack of intimacy as a positive, masculine trait, as it suggests a lack of vulnerability. Men are often likely to see a sexual dysfunction as more embarrassing or problematic than a lack of intimacy.

With women, intimacy is generally understood to be emotional openness. While sex might be physically satisfying, there is no emotional connection beyond the pleasure. Without intimacy, there is no difference between having sex with an anonymous stranger (or even masturbating) and having sex with a spouse. Again, as with men, a lack of sexual desire could be a symptom of diminished intimacy, as well as a cause for it. Without becoming too graphic, many women will opt to "fake" interest in sex so as not to let on that there is a problem, an option not as easily available to men. Of course, women can also make the shortcut between sex and intimacy, perhaps using sex to "solve" disagreements or distract themselves and their partners from other issues. Obviously, this sort of "make-up sex" doesn't truly solve any problems and is simply another form of denial.

While learning to communicate with a partner about your feelings is an important step in building intimacy, it shouldn't be assumed that intimacy means lots of talking. In fact, many healthy couples don't have a lot of verbal communication. This is because a part of emotional honesty involves understanding when nothing needs to be said at all.

As with the other pillars, a lack of intimacy doesn't necessarily stand in the way of building a relationship. In fact, many relationships without intimacy can last for years or even decades without either partner even realizing that anything is wrong. But without intimacy, what you generally have is a strong friendship rather than a truly loving relationship. It's the reason why some people can step into and out of one relationship after another without seeming to suffer much emotional damage. It's why some people are able to remarry within months of a spouse dying, simply because the loss of that individual didn't cost them too much emotionally.

And how do people learn to build intimacy? Ironically, they might need to speak with a therapist, psychiatrist, counselor, or spiritual advisor, such as a priest, rabbi, or minister. I've dealt with a lot of couples who had to open up to me before they could open up to someone they'd already known for years. Sometimes, people need the emotional safety of speaking to a relative stranger; since we're not friends, it essentially doesn't matter what I think of them. Other times, someone needs "permission" to open up to another person. Of course, when dealing with intimacy issues, people are going to make themselves vulnerable, and a potential danger is that a spouse and a counselor bringing up a problem will give the impression that they're "ganging up" on the other spouse when they're in that vulnerable state. Building intimacy involves both making yourself vulnerable and being protective of a partner.

Carlos and Kathy

While Carlos didn't grow up in an abusive environment, he still encountered issues that would make it difficult for him to develop intimacy later in life. His parents divorced when he was ten years old, and he had little contact with his father after that point. In addition, he had an older brother and younger sister, which gave him problems unique to middle children. His mother was a nurse and was able to provide Carlos with a middle-class upbringing, so he had no financial hardships. But being raised by a single working parent, with two other children who also needed attention, meant that Carlos was effectively neglected for much of his childhood. He soon learned how to do many things on his own, as did his older brother and younger sister, becoming self-sufficient at a younger age than most people. While this self-sufficiency brought on a greater maturity, it also made him less prone to reach out to others for help and less prone to depend on others when help was offered.

By contrast, Kathy was the only child of a loving couple who didn't divorce. She was raised with a steady example of an adult couple that trusted one another and freely expressed their emotions with each other and with her. For Kathy, emotional openness was not a burden and didn't require a terrible risk.

As an adult, Carlos became an IT consultant for a major corporation. He was socially active and dated frequently. He'd entered into a number of relationships and, while pleasant, they never lasted for longer than eight to nine months. Though abuse and infidelity were not a part of these relationships, for some reason that he couldn't understand, none of the relationships he'd entered could last for even a year.

Like Carlos, Kathy also had a number of close friends. But while she'd dated, she'd never been in a serious, long-term relationship before meeting him. She was employed as a chemical engineer, so needed no financial support. And her family provided her with emotional support. Still, she wanted to find someone to share her life.

Eventually, the two of them met on a dating website. Both were outgoing. Both shared similar religious beliefs. Both of them wanted to have children. Both of them were interested in a long-term relationship. They seemed like an ideal couple according to the metrics set up by the dating website, as well as to the casual observer. Carlos was Kathy's first long-term relationship, while Kathy was Carlos's first relationship to last longer than a year. Eventually, they got married.

As with so many of the troubled couples that have come to me for help, their relationship looked fine from the outside. There was no abuse, they rarely argued, and no infidelity. And even when they realized that something was wrong, they still had difficulty articulating what exactly was missing. Carlos wasn't behaving any differently than he'd behaved in any of his past relationships, save that this one had resulted in marriage rather than simply ending. Kathy had never been in a serious relationship before Carlos, so she had no point of reference to judge their relationship.

They'd both learned to change their mindsets enough to be open to a long-term relationship. They trusted one another. And they had no trouble communicating with one another.

What was missing from their relationship was intimacy. Carlos had long equated intimacy with sex, so he would not have thought intimacy was the problem since their sexual relationship seemed healthy. And while Kathy found the sex unsatisfying, she had trouble articulating that it was a lack of intimacy that left her feeling disconnected from the act (keeping in mind that she had little prior sexual experience for comparison).

When they came to see me, I helped them narrow down the problem to issues with intimacy. Of course, Carlos immediately assumed that I meant sex when referring to intimacy, while Kathy assured me that they did love each other, so the three of us needed to have a conversation about what was actually missing in their relationship. Once I explained that lack of intimacy didn't mean a lack of sex or a lack of love, but rather a lack of emotional vulnerability, they were more receptive to working on the problem. After that, they completed a series of exercises designed to increase their emotional honesty with one another.

One of the easiest exercises was for Carlos to simply hold Kathy in silence for a minute before saying something positive to her. Another activity was establishing "date nights" where they would spend time together. Unlike typical dates, however, they would spend these nights at home, talking with one another, rather than going out and focusing on a movie, concert, or special event. Couples who are both outgoing and lead active social lives often lack basic intimacy; many times, they use social activities to fill up their spare time so that they don't have to be alone with each other.

I also suggested that the two of them keep a love journal (similar to the one I had Lewis and Abigail do), in which each of them would write something nice about the other on a daily basis. While this was an entirely new practice for Carlos, Kathy had already been keeping a journal of her personal experiences since she was a child.

Some resistance is common from one or both partners during counseling. Perhaps only one of them sees the problem or perhaps one of them finds the exercises I suggest to be meaningless or uncomfortable. In this case, Carlos and Kathy both took to the exercises instantly and found them to be quite enjoyable.

While they've been making progress toward increased intimacy, the changes can be slow, since Carlos is working with long-ingrained habits. So I still meet with them both on a monthly basis.

William

There's an old saying about being "married to your job." We've all met a few people who seem genuinely reluctant to go home to their families, preferring to spend nights and weekends at the office or on the road. Whether this behavior comes from a genuine love for one's job or as an effort to avoid domestic problems, the result is the same: relationships suffer.

Perhaps these "dedicated" employees are willing to change their mindsets to accommodate a new situation. Perhaps they're willing to trust another person enough to let them share their lives. Perhaps there's nothing wrong with their communication skills. But the simple act of not being physically present will destroy any intimacy that might have developed. You can't build intimacy through nothing more than daily text messages and vacations twice a year.

Of course, when William was growing up, he wouldn't have understood the complex requirements of an emotional relationship. What he knew was that both of his parents were successful people. William's father was raised to believe that the man should be the sole breadwinner of the family, so he dedicated himself to a job that would provide enough money for himself and his wife. William's mother, on the other hand, didn't want to be financially dependent on her husband, so she pursued a career of her own. Both of them worked long hours, saw each other infrequently, and had no problem with that arrangement.

However, when William was born, their situation changed dramatically. Neither of them had planned to have children, and while they weren't physically or verbally abusive toward their son, they also made no effort to hide the fact that he wasn't wanted. William was treated and felt like a burden all his life, and his parents dealt with that burden by passing him off to babysitters and childcare services as often as possible so their careers wouldn't get sidetracked by caring for him. While he wasn't thrown out of their house and his basic needs were met, William was emotionally abandoned.

Without nurturing parents, William simply never developed emotionally. He did well in school but formed few friendships. Eventually, he became a successful criminal defense attorney. But despite being intelligent and successful, William was unable to maintain a relationship for longer than six months.

Again, one of the biggest problems with a toxic upbringing is that, to the child being raised, it all seems normal. Children generally have only one point of reference for how a family should work, and that's the family that they're in. Without any obvious physical abuse, William likely believed that his parents behaved the way most normal adults did. Of course, he understood that they resented him, but he reached the assumption that there must be something wrong with him and that he deserved that resentment. Eventually, William isolated himself from others because of the resulting low self-esteem. The fact that none of the relationships he formed could last for more than a handful of months only reinforced the belief that there must be something wrong with him (and not with his ideas about how to maintain a relationship).

William finally sought counseling when he was thirty-three years old, which is how he first met with me. Initially, I'm sure that he was expecting me to simply explain what was "wrong" with him. After so many years, he might have suspected that whatever was wrong with him couldn't be fixed, that it might even be some form of mental illness.

It didn't take long for me to understand the actual problem and explain to William that there was nothing inherently "wrong" with him. He simply needed some help learning how to foster intimacy. His immediate reaction was relief. After that, he was extremely receptive to the exercises I suggested.

The first exercise was to simply go to a shopping mall and strike up a conversation with a stranger. This exercise is similar to the one that I suggested to Judy and is similar to exercises that I suggest to many of my clients. Shopping malls are great places to find a wide variety of different people, and the many activities going on make it easy to casually comment on something in order to open up a conversation. As with Judy, the shopping mall exercise was simply intended to help William improve his social skills. He wasn't trying to get a stranger's phone numbers or otherwise "hook up." By keeping the conversations light and inconsequential, William removed a lot of the pressure he might have otherwise felt to form a serious relationship rather than simply enjoy somebody's company.

Before we'd begun our sessions together, William essentially had no social life outside of his job. He would work, go home, and do little else. Home became the safe place where he wouldn't be judged and wouldn't be a problem for anyone else. While he wasn't an actual agoraphobic, he certainly had a reluctance to visit unfamiliar places or interact with unfamiliar people. Getting out anywhere, even to a shopping mall, widened the area where he felt safe.

It might seem odd that an attorney would have difficulty in social situations. In fact, it's not uncommon for someone to be comfortable, even talkative, in a professional setting, but suddenly tight-lipped when things become less formal. In some ways, the lack of a rigid social code can be intimidating. Without clear rules about what is and isn't appropriate to discuss or a business matter to focus on, many people find themselves uncertain about what to say and panic about possibly saying the wrong thing.

Once William's confidence with non-work-related conversation had increased, he was ready to try another exercise. While his parents had never been overtly abusive, the neglect he'd suffered had nevertheless left some serious emotional damage. As he'd grown older, William contacted his parents less and less often until, at thirty-three, he was virtually a stranger to them. His next exercise was to try repairing the relationship with his parents. Initially, he simply met them for dinner once in a while. Like the mall conversations, this exercise worked only if it was handled in a casual manner. William did not accuse his parents of neglecting him and didn't even mention that he had sought counseling for his intimacy issues. Instead, he concentrated only on talking with them.

At first, William's father remained cold and distant, but over time began to open up more toward his son. Part of the shift in attitude probably came as his father realized that he no longer had to treat William like a child who needed him. William was an adult who could take care of himself, so his father had no reason to treat him like a burden. Eventually, the two of them began taking golf lessons together and, if they're not a model for a father-son relationship, they've at least become friends.

William's relationship with his mother is still cold, but he continues to meet with her for dinner.

Once William had learned better social skills through his mall visits and begun repairing childhood emotional damage by speaking with his parents, it was time for him to begin working on future relationships. He joined a church and made several friends there. I've often suggested that my clients find a church or other religious organization to join. Not only do churches provide new social opportunities, but they also provide various ways for individuals to interact with their communities.

As of this writing, William still meets with me every other month, mostly to update me on his progress and seek advice on his continuing attempts to be more open with people. Recently, he's begun a relationship with a woman he's met at his church. While they've only gone on a handful of dates so far, he's already opening up more to her than he's done to women in his previous relationships

Action Steps

I mentioned earlier how many people will mistake sexual compatibility for intimacy. I see this assumption play out every time I suggest to a couple that they might have a lack of intimacy in their relationship. Often I'm met with the response that, oh no, "there's nothing wrong with that." Once I explain that intimacy refers more to emotional vulnerability than to sexual fulfillment, there will still be some confusion from people who assume that you can't have the latter without the former. A healthy sex life is not a sure indicator of emotional intimacy, and a lack of intimacy can't be fixed by having more sex.

But the sex=intimacy assumption isn't the only misconception about this relationship key essential. Another common assumption is that romance and intimacy are the same thing. Like sex, romance doesn't guarantee a healthy level of intimacy. In fact, many romantic ideas and gestures are detrimental to a relationship. Too much romance can actually destroy a relationship.

It seems counterintuitive that romance can damage a relationship since romance novels and romantic films invariably end with a relationship being formed. But the problem with this concept is that those stories always end with the relationship just beginning, and a healthy relationship isn't going to stay at that starting stage. Believing that your partner is the smartest, kindest, most attractive, and most wonderful person you know sounds like a great foundation, but the truth is that nobody can ever live up to those romantic standards.

We are flawed beings, and we love flawed beings. One of the problems I encounter over and over again is this idea of the perfect partner—men and women looking for the perfect partner and remaining alone because those perfect partners can't be found. Men and women trying to be the perfect partner and isolating themselves because they can never measure up to such standards. And worst of all, the fact that even if someone honestly seems like a "perfect match" for you, that person will change in the years and decades to come into someone quite different . . . just like you will do. Romance doesn't take those changes into account, often glossing it over with the words "happily ever after."

So, obviously, one action step is to consciously separate romantic fantasy from relationship reality. Accept that, despite your partner's flaws, he or she is still worthy of love. And accept that, despite your flaws, you too are worthy of love. By accepting these two truths, you'll start to deal with the fear that we all feel when we become more intimate: the idea that, if someone got to know us as we "really are," they would never love us. By accepting the flaws of others, you make it easier to accept your own flaws . . . and make it easier for others to accept those flaws as well.

But accepting flaws and maintaining an emotional vulnerability isn't something that you can do once and then stop. Again, that's the romantic notion of the one grand gesture. Intimacy is something that we each have to work to maintain. And there are a number of special action steps each of us can take to either maintain the intimacy in a relationship or keep ourselves emotionally open to others.

I've mentioned setting up "date nights" already, but it's an important cornerstone of the relationship that bears repeating. It's how most of our relationships begin: by setting aside a special time to spend with another person. As the relationship matures, however, we start to allot less time for things like dates. After all, why spend any more time getting to know someone we've married? Don't we already know them well enough? Again, people change over time, and the only way to continue a relationship is to be aware of those changes; otherwise, you will wake up one day and realize that your husband or wife has been replaced by a stranger.

Unlike the dates we normally go on at the beginning of a relationship, these date nights don't have to be anything elaborate or expensive. In fact, a concert or movie makes a poor choice at that stage because the event will be the focus instead of the person joining you. Consider a dinner at a quiet restaurant or an outdoor picnic for two. Or just turn off your phones for a few hours and spend some uninterrupted time with one another at home. Even going grocery shopping together can become an opportunity for intimacy. The options are many, as long as your partner is the focus of the date.

Of course, there are going to be times when we don't have a few hours to spare. Either our schedules are packed so tightly or our jobs take us out of town for weeks at a time or we're simply too exhausted at the end of the day to do anything but fall asleep. Both partners working full time, especially if they both have demanding careers, can create serious problems for maintaining intimacy in a relationship. And while I will often recommend trying to carve time out of a busy schedule for relationship activities, that sometimes isn't possible. At those times, I recommend at least making a weekly check-in. These don't have to be chunks of hours carved out of a day. They can be a phone call during a lunch break or simply a conversation in bed before both of you go to sleep. The important thing is to conduct the check-ins on a regular basis so you maintain some emotional connection.

In the end, maintaining intimacy needs to be about more than simply saving a relationship. In fact, plenty of relationships can run for a lifetime with no intimacy at all, but those relationships are never fulfilling ("marriage of convenience" is a term that still gets used to describe too many modern relationships). When you make yourself emotionally vulnerable to another person, you open yourself to a validation that more timid people never get; you open yourself to being accepted for who you truly are. And you are able to provide the same reassurance to someone you love, provided they take the same risk to open themselves to you.

Chapter 6

Conflict Resolution

The fifth and final key essential for maintaining a healthy relationship is conflict resolution. As with all of the other key essentials, there is more to conflict resolution than most people realize. First of all, learning conflict resolution skills is not synonymous with learning to compromise. While compromise is certainly one element of conflict resolution, it's far from the only element. In fact, a willingness to compromise isn't even the most vital element of conflict resolution.

The most vital element to conflict resolution is simply the desire to end the conflict. Chances are that you've been involved in at least one argument where the other person concedes that you were right, yet you felt somehow dissatisfied with simply "winning" the fight. While you won on a certain level, you're still angry and still want to fight, but now you have nothing to fight about.

I've encountered many couples that will argue seemingly for nothing more than the sake of arguing. In many cases, the subject of the argument is simply used as a cover for some deeper issue that neither partner wishes to acknowledge. For example, an argument over where to go on a vacation might mask a deeper problem, such as one partner wanting to move to a new city and the other partner wanting to stay where they are. In other cases, a disagreement is settled in a way that is unsatisfactory to one or both partners so that they continue arguing over a problem that's already been "solved."

While anger is a toxic emotion, it's also an addictive state of mind. When we're angry, we're often more confident that we're right and other people are wrong. Feeling angry often seems preferable to thinking that we're wrong. We also feel more energized when we're angry than when we're sad or frightened. While spiritually damaging in the long run, many people will choose to feed their anger rather than resolve it in a way that might leave them feeling weak or defeated. Unfortunately, this anger is often fed at the expense of an otherwise stable relationship.

Michael and Stephanie

We've all watched television programs with eternally bickering couples. Such arguments are designed to maintain a sense of drama on a weekly basis. And every week, the arguments are either resolved at the end of the episode or some indication is given that the partners truly love one another, despite all of the arguing. And while it's true that any couple will argue from time to time, the message that too many of us have gleaned from such programs is that constant arguing is a sign of a healthy relationship. After all, arguing with someone shows that you care what that person thinks, and arguing is certainly better than not communicating at all.

Michael and Stephanie both grew up believing that arguing equaled healthy communication. Of course, their behavior was modeled more after their respective parents than television couples. Both of them grew up in homes where their parents were verbally and emotionally abusive. In both cases, the parents' abuse was aimed solely at one another and not toward their children. In some ways, not being subjected to abuse only reinforced the toxic message even further, as it showed that arguing was something that adults did with one another when they were in a relationship. Their parents weren't abusive toward everyone, only toward each other, so it would seem to the children that abuse was something that you only did when in a relationship with someone.

Furthermore, since the abuse was never physical, both children were presented with a false moral line that hitting was abuse, but yelling and insulting was not. So both Michael and Stephanie grew up believing that insulting someone's intelligence or appearance wasn't abuse. Screaming at someone wasn't abuse. Threatening to leave someone wasn't abuse. As long as nobody was punched or slapped, then no abuse was taking place, and in fact all of these things were healthy expressions of opinion.

Michael and Stephanie both grew up to be teachers and worked at the same school. They dated for ten months before getting married. While similar upbringings and similar values usually contribute to a healthy marriage, in this case their similar attitudes toward conflict resolution quickly led to serious problems.

The arguments began immediately after they were married. I've mentioned already that marriage is different than dating and that the dynamic of a couple can change significantly once they're married. In this case, Michael and Stephanie didn't live together until after they got married, so they had the added stress that comes with adjusting to living with someone.

But the real problem was that both partners saw conflict as a measuring stick of whether or not they were in a good relationship. They didn't understand that all couples experience conflict for the simple reason that conflict will always exist where there are differences between people. To them, conflict was a sign of something wrong with the relationship, the only way to solve the conflict was to communicate, and the only way to communicate was through arguing.

Like their parents, Michael and Stephanie would call one another names, accuse one another of not listening, and blame one another for not understanding their feelings. They perfectly mirrored the toxic behavior they'd observed during their early years. However, unlike their parents, they soon felt overwhelmed and realized that constant arguing wasn't going to keep them together.

Unlike their parents, they hadn't yet had any children, so at least a new generation wasn't learning these bad relationship habits. Having no children was a conscious choice, as they didn't want to strain their relationship even more with the demands of child-rearing. Ironically, many dysfunctional couples have the opposing view that children will bring them closer together. But Michael and Stephanie chose to not have children because the relationship would be easier to dissolve if things didn't work out. Before the marriage had even happened, they'd essentially made themselves an exit strategy.

After only one month of marriage, they sought counseling. Again, Michael and Stephanie were not the first couple to realize quickly after marriage that their relationship needed help.

The first thing I needed to help them understand is that the presence of conflict doesn't instantly make a relationship "bad." In fact, the ways couples handle such conflict indicates whether or not a relationship is functional. In many cases, the conflicts can be traced toward a problem with one of the other relationship key essentials—an unwillingness to change one's mindset, a lack of trust, a lack of communication, or a lack of intimacy. In their case, the issue was largely based on a lack of trust.

Specifically, this couple had issues regarding two different but significant types of trust. First, each had trouble trusting the other with their emotional well-being, meaning that neither was certain the other wouldn't try to hurt them if they showed vulnerability. Second, neither trusted the other's judgment, so that even if they believed their partner had the best of intentions, they didn't trust their spouse to make the correct decision. We've all met people who win people's trust just so that they can hurt them. We've also all met people who are always trying to help, yet who always end up making things worse despite their good intentions.

So some of Michael and Stephanie's relationship-building activities were based around building trust. They had to trust one another's intentions, and they also had to trust one another's competence.

Beyond trust issues, Michael and Stephanie needed to learn how to deal with conflict in more constructive ways. When they first approached me, any conflict situation quickly escalated into an argument, and every argument grew to a "fight to the death" level of intensity. Although like their parents, Michael and Stephanie's arguments never crossed a line to physical abuse, they both needed help keeping their emotions in check.

One simple tool I gave them for de-escalating arguments was the idea of using a "password." The idea is that, during an argument, either of them can say a word that will immediately stop the argument. After the argument is stopped, both of them agree to separate for forty-five minutes, get their emotions under control, then reconnect. Once they both have a "cooldown" period, they each own up to what they did to cause the conflict and what they did to escalate matters. Then, with cooler heads, they work together to find a solution.

The password system provides an excellent example of how Michael and Stephanie had to learn to trust each other on two different levels. While the setup seems straightforward enough, the potential for abuse, intentional or not, is significant. For example, one of them could use the password whenever he or she was losing an argument, essentially shutting up the partner whenever they wanted. A password could also become an unintentional method for avoiding important but uncomfortable truths by misinterpreting "not wanting to hear" something as "abuse." The password system required each partner trusting the other not to intentionally misuse it, as well as trusting one another to understand the difference between honesty and abuse.

Of course, habits learned over a lifetime aren't changed after a single session. As of this writing, it's been eight months since I first met with Michael and Stephanie. They still meet with me on a regular basis and, while they've made great progress, they both acknowledge that they still have a lot of work to do in improving both themselves and their relationship.

Carl

Most of the people who come to see me realize they have a problem. Maybe they don't understand exactly what's wrong. Maybe they think they have one problem when they really have a different problem. If it's a couple, perhaps each partner suspects that the other one has the problem. Whatever the case, most of the time, when people come to see me, they at least realize that something is wrong. We can at least agree that there is a problem and then work together to clarify the issue and the solution.

But sometimes my clients don't even realize they have a problem.

Like many of my clients, Carl's troubles could be traced back to a childhood filled with abuse. Carl's parents were both verbally and physically abusive toward one another, and he frequently witnessed them getting into fistfights with one another. Furthermore, his parents were also verbally and physically abusive toward him. Like so many children raised in abusive households, Carl grew up believing that this sort of behavior was normal and that physical violence was an acceptable means of dealing with conflict.

As a child, Carl was physically small. In addition to the abuse he suffered from his parents at home, he was also abused by children, both verbally and physically, at school. Teachers and school faculty never intervened on his behalf but can't be held totally accountable for their lack of involvement. Children are often hesitant to report such abuse to adults, partially out of embarrassment and partially from fear of reprisals. Many teachers are so overworked and concerned with more obvious problems that they miss subtle cues. And children can be surprisingly adept at hiding bruises and other signs of physical abuse. Since Carl was abused by both of his parents and no one in his family was taking action, he had no reason to believe that any other adults would offer help if he reached out to them, either. So for most of Carl's childhood, he was essentially in a survival mode.

The sad truth about children who get through abuse by approaching everyone with suspicion, withdrawing emotionally, and staying in a perpetual fight-or-flight mode of thinking . . . is that those strategies can actually work. Children aren't able to simply leave abusive relationships with their parents. They can't physically overwhelm them, and they are often not believed when they seek out help. Even if someone does believe them and they are removed from abusive households, resources are limited and foster families aren't plentiful enough to accommodate all of the children escaping abuse. So learning to normalize the abuse is sometimes the best—though admittedly still terrible—option that many of these children have available.

Unfortunately, when these children grow up, those habits don't change without effort. And if a strategy has worked for their entire lives, they may not see the need to change once they reach a certain age. And it's not as if adults don't face conflicts as well.

So when Carl left home at age seventeen, he went to college without ever developing healthy social skills. Unsurprisingly, he had few friends in college, still going day-to-day in that same survival mode, despite the fact that his parents and the school bullies were no longer a part of his life. He did well academically—not being distracted with a lot of social obligations—and after graduation got a job as an engineer.

This isn't to say that Carl never dated or didn't make attempts at forming romantic relationships. It's just that he couldn't let go of his anger, even in relationships with no abuse. Conflict and disagreements invariably come, and the only methods he had learned to deal with conflict were verbal and physical abuse. All of his relationships became explosive because of this reaction to conflict.

When he was a child, the abuse that Carl suffered was entirely the fault of his parents or other children. At the time, he was too small to defend himself, and despite normalizing such abuse, he still understood that he wasn't to blame in such situations. Unfortunately, he maintained this attitude into adulthood, blaming the women in his relationships for the horrible arguments that would inevitably ensue between them. When he got into arguments with coworkers or other people, he always found a way to blame them for the conflicts escalating. What began as a clear understanding of a child's powerlessness became a toxic habit of blaming other people for his behavior as an adult.

Of course, there are other ways for adults to deal with conflict situations, even situations where the other person is growing verbally or physically abusive. They can put some temporary distance between themselves and the other person. They can also call for help.

During one especially heated argument Carl had with a woman, he went beyond verbal abuse and became physically abusive toward her as well. The physical abuse didn't escalate beyond roughly pushing her, but it was enough for her to contact the police. Carl later told me that this was the first time an argument had escalated from shouting and insults to physical pushing, but at the time he didn't see how he had crossed a moral line.

Carl was arrested and spent a night in jail. Again, at the time, he probably didn't understand why "simply" pushing his girlfriend warranted such a reaction. But the simple fact is that the police and the court officers deal with many cases of domestic abuse, and they see how simple actions can escalate if not addressed. The police will visit the same residences over and over again, watching as shoving escalates to punching, and punching escalates to attacks with knives, guns, or other weapons. And when those incidents are recounted in courtrooms, the judges and attorneys see the escalation as well.

When Carl met with a judge, he was told that there wouldn't be a trial. Given Carl's lack of any previous criminal record, the judge had decided that it would be best if he agreed to six months' worth of weekly counseling sessions specifically aimed at anger management issues. Carl would otherwise be free to go. However, if he skipped his counseling sessions or physically attacked anyone else, fresh charges would be brought against him and he would likely end up in jail. The judge directed him to speak with a counselor with extensive experience in dealing with anger management issues, especially those rooted in childhood abuse.

That is how I found myself speaking with a client who didn't want to see me and didn't believe that he had any problems. At first, the sessions were nonproductive, to say the least. Most of the time, Carl would merely sit in my office throughout our scheduled sessions, saying little or nothing. He made it clear that he believed the mandatory counseling wasn't necessary and he intended to fulfill the letter of the agreement by sitting in my office for the required number of sessions, but he saw no reason to even try fixing a problem that he didn't believe existed.

I could have simply gone through the motions with Carl as well. After all, if someone doesn't want help, there isn't much that anyone else can do to force the issue. I had plenty of other clients who were actively seeking help, even if they didn't quite understand the problems they faced. I could have asked him the same series of questions every week, gotten the same series of vague answers, and ticked a number off his list of required sessions until we were both finished.

But I chose instead to try something different. Standard sessions only worked for people who wanted help. So if Carl didn't want help, then I would need to try something different.

I invited Carl to go out to lunch with me instead of just sitting in my office. Since he had no interest in traditional counseling, he welcomed the chance to fulfill his legal obligations by having lunch in a restaurant rather than sitting in an office answering the same questions over and over again. After that, we spent our session times going to movies, golfing, and learning to relax around one another. At some point, I finally gained his trust by being his friend rather than his court-appointed counselor. Given what I eventually learned about Carl's upbringing and how difficult it was for him to form friendships, I was honored that he chose to trust me.

And here's where I had to take all of the advice that I'd been giving to other people and apply it to myself as well. Because in order for my relationship with Carl to be a true friendship, I needed to place some trust in him and show a willingness to have honest communication. So I gave him a copy of my first book, Messed Up and Don't Even Know It: The Journey from Childhood Trauma to Healing. The book outlines several cases of childhood abuse and how each child grew up with emotional baggage and toxic behavior patterns. In each case, I presented steps for how one could deal with the aftermath of abuse.

The reason that giving Carl this book was an act of trust on my part was that one of those stories of childhood abuse was my own.

There was a chance that reading about the abuse I suffered as a child might have closed Carl off from further communication. Perhaps he would decide that I was still messed up from the abuse and in no position to help anyone else. That risk required trust on my part.

As it turned out, giving him the book led to a breakthrough in his treatment. Far from alienating him, my book helped him understand that I wasn't merely an outsider looking in on him. I understood how strange it could seem that the coping mechanisms that had served so well in childhood were now causing problems in adulthood. It might well have been like being dropped on an alien world, where all of the rules and standards you'd known all of your life were no longer observed by anyone else. It was like having to learn right from wrong all over again.

Once Carl trusted me, it was easier for me to point out that he was still angry about things that had happened to him decades ago. And while he was entitled to his anger, he was taking it out on people who had nothing to do with the abuse that he had suffered years earlier. Not every disagreement had to escalate into an argument, as they had with his parents, and arguments never had to escalate into abuse, either verbal or physical. It was easier to point out the mistakes he was making because I had made many of them myself, so our conversations were less about lecturing him about right and wrong and more about helping him find a path that I'd already had to walk myself.

Once we'd come to trust one another, Carl and I began discussing the roots of his aggressive behavior. By pointing out that what he'd gone through as a child was abuse, it was easier to show that this behavior was not normal or acceptable. And while his reactions to it were understandable, the habits he'd developed were no longer serving him well in his adult life. At that point, I began to suggest other ways that he might handle conflict situations.

One simple method was to simply walk away from a hostile situation, something he hadn't been able to do as a child. Whether he was becoming abusive or the other person was becoming abusive, walking away for a brief time would allow him time to look at the situation from a less immediate and emotional perspective. Walking away could also protect Carl and other people physically by placing literal distance between them before confrontations became violent. I also recommended that Carl take time to simply count before he spoke; even the minute it took to count could be enough to cool off a sudden temper. In the same way, I suggested that he write things down before he said them, which worked especially well if he was planning to start an argument rather than suddenly finding himself in the middle of one. Each of these techniques offered ways for Carl to pause and objectively consider his words and actions.

I also wanted Carl to take steps to reduce his stress level. I encouraged him to begin exercising more regularly. I also advised him to get more sleep by going to bed earlier. Regular exercise, increased sleep, and a healthier diet not only reduce stress levels but also decrease the risk of other health problems, which can, in turn, reduce stress levels even further.

Since I'd taken the time to get to know Carl and trusted him enough to let him get to know me as well, he was far more receptive to all of my suggestions. And while forming friendships with all of my clients isn't a practical option, in this case it produced positive results.

At the time of this writing, Carl has finished his series of court-appointed sessions; however, he still maintains a regular monthly appointment schedule with me. He isn't involved in a relationship at the moment, recognizing that he still needs to do a lot of work on his conflict resolution skills before he can be a supportive and emotionally open partner. Part of this work involves coming to terms with his past. While he does maintain some communication with his abusive parents, repairing that relationship is still very much a work in progress.

Action Steps

No matter your religious beliefs or what type of ceremony you observed when getting married, marriage is primarily a spiritual union rather than a physical one. Since all people are different, conflicts will naturally arise in relationships, since it's through conflict that we reveal our differences to one another. More than anything else, marriage should be viewed as an instrument for smoothing over those conflicts without suppressing our differences. One of the worst things you can do in a marriage—or any other relationship—is to pretend that no differences exist in order to avoid conflict, or "going along to get along." But when conflicts do arise, you want to make sure that you work through them without becoming abusive or suffering abuse. Your partner is the person who should be helping you resolve the conflict and not an enemy to be conquered.

With all of that said, how should one resolve conflicts properly? People raised in abusive households have certainly seen their share of bad conflict resolution strategies, and while those strategies may yield some short-term gains, in the long term they can ruin our current relationships and make it difficult or impossible to foster new and healthy ones in the future. I try to tailor conflict resolution strategies to each individual or couple that I meet, focusing on their specific issues. However, I've found four tools that tend to work for most people—in and out of relationships—who are having trouble with conflict resolution: humility, open-mindedness, compromise, and forgiveness.

The first tool to consider is humility. The simplest definition of humility is an absence of self. While most of us like to believe that we can be objective, the fact is that we all want things to go our way. How often have we had to admonish someone with the phrase, "It's not all about you"? How many times has someone said those words to us? How many times have we gotten into arguments where we suddenly realized we were wrong, but rather than simply admitting it, we chose instead to continue the argument? When we do these things, we'll often say things like "it was the principle of the thing" or "it wasn't about being right, but being treated with respect." But oftentimes these are just excuses for a lack of humility. Without humility, we get into arguments simply because somebody tells us that we're wrong, and not to defend a principle.

Of course, we're not always able to even acknowledge that we could be wrong. Many people have grown up doing things one way and see no reason to change, even if someone they love tries doing things a different way. Couples have gotten into arguments over religion, political ideologies, where to live, and whether or not to have children. But they've also gotten into violent and relationship-ending arguments over far more frivolous issues. How many of us have met a couple who gets into a shouting match over what to have for dinner, what to watch on television, or what color bedsheets to buy? We've all seen these people in stores, in restaurants, and on the street, having their arguments over the silliest issues.

But the next time you find yourself in an argument, consider how frivolous it might seem to an outside observer. And then ask yourself what the person you're arguing with must be thinking. Why are they arguing as passionately as you? What makes them so convinced that they're right and you're wrong? What if the way you've always done something is in fact NOT the best way to do something? Many of the clients I've described in earlier chapters only began to make progress when they became open minded enough to consider alternative ways of doing things. When communicating with a partner, an open-minded person needs to offer constructive criticism that doesn't degrade or downplay the importance of the other person's ideas. At the same time, the open-minded person needs to be receptive toward constructive, nonabusive criticism of their own ideas. Keep in mind that, in order for open-mindedness to work, both partners need to keep an open mind; otherwise, it will just degenerate into one partner making themselves vulnerable to abuse by the other.

Of course, once people learn to stop placing their own needs ahead of anyone else's and keep an open mind to the possibility that they might not be right about everything, the next step is to begin compromising. It's surprising how many conflicts in relationships can be resolved by either finding a middle ground or letting each partner do things their own way. Of course, I should probably stress at this point that there are issues where compromise should not be an option. In cases where one partner wants to do something illegal or unethical, it is the responsibility of the other partner to maintain an ethical position. But if you're honest with yourself, you probably never get into fights with your partner about whether or not they should start a drug dealing business or cheat on their taxes. It's more likely something such as where you want to go on vacation this year or who you should invite to a party. In most cases, it's to everyone's benefit if you move off your position, consider other positions, and try finding a solution agreeable to both of you.

Finally, there is the tool of forgiveness. I'd love to say that it's possible to simply use this tool without spending time on humility, open-mindedness, and compromise. But the fact is that all of those other tools need to be used before forgiveness is possible. If you don't believe me, then think back to a time when someone apologized and you instantly accepted that apology. Maybe you'd gone through all of those other steps in your mind long before the apology came, but more likely you simply accepted the apology in order to put the whole conflict behind you. But without humility, you're still angry that someone so close to you would question your judgment. Without open-mindedness, you still think that you were completely in the right and the other person was completely in the wrong. Without compromise, you've made no effort to find a middle ground on the issue, so that a new argument will simply flare up the next time that issue comes up. Without humility, open-mindedness, and compromise, forgiveness is simply a series of hollow words that keep conflict buried for a brief time. On the other hand, when all four tools are used together, forgiveness can end with a true canceling of emotional debts on both sides.

An analogy that I like to use is that marriage is like a precious vase. One of the things that makes it beautiful is its fragility. When we meet a couple who have been married for fifty years, we aren't amazed by the strength of the marriage, but rather by the two individuals who've managed to keep something so delicate together for so long. So many things can end a marriage, and make no mistake, some things absolutely should end certain marriages. Nobody should stay in a marriage that's abusive, especially if the partner has rejected multiple opportunities to cease the abusive behavior.

But like a precious vase, sometimes something happens that causes it to shatter. It could be verbal abuse. It could be an affair. It could be a secret that should have been shared but was instead discovered some other way. It could be physical abuse. Whatever the case, something changes the relationship significantly, often to the point where it is effectively "broken."

And in some cases—especially those where one or both partners are unwilling to acknowledge their mistakes or change their behaviors—a marriage may well be better off simply ending. But since few people file for divorce in haste, what happens instead is that the couple stays together, maintaining the marriage but also continuing the abusive treatment that broke it. To use the vase analogy again, if you break a vase once, it's possible to glue the pieces back together, if that's what you want to do. But if you deal with a broken vase by systematically breaking every piece even further until there's nothing left but powder, then it's truly beyond repair.

In the same way, many marriages can be salvaged if both partners acknowledge the problems early enough. But if the problems are left to linger and the abusive treatment continues for too long, the relationship degenerates into something that's truly beyond anyone's ability to salvage.

Chapter 7

Conclusion

No two relationships are the same. This is because no two people are the same, obviously, but the differences go even deeper than the people involved. Relationships change over time. Parents' relationships with their children can go from caregivers to counselors to friends as those children become adults and no longer need caregivers. The dynamics of a marriage change drastically once husband and wife become father and mother to a child. A serious illness can thrust one partner into the role of caregiver. A former stay-at-home parent reentering the professional world will thrust the other partner out of the role as sole provider. Tragedy can transform one or both partners into emotional custodians. So even the same two people can end up having several different types of relationship with one another over the course of decades.

But in each type of relationship, the same five key essentials are necessary. Both partners need to remain open to changing their mindsets as the nature of the relationship shifts and outside conditions force change. Both partners need to maintain trust with one another, otherwise they'll slowly drift apart emotionally, even if they continue living under the same roof. They both need to routinely communicate with one another, remembering to listen at least as much they speak. They both need to work at maintaining intimacy, willing to make themselves emotionally vulnerable and respect the other's vulnerability. And they need to develop effective conflict resolution skills to cope with the inevitable differences that will exist between them as they both continue to grow and change.

But the key essentials are like any other sort of skill. Some people will have a natural aptitude for them, while others will struggle to learn the basics. Some people have been taught them at an early age through the example of a stable household, while others won't have a childhood example to model. In fact, many of us grow up in dysfunctional families and, when it comes to maintaining relationships, we learn the wrong way to do it. And like any other skill, some of us continue practicing, while others learn just enough of a skill to "get by."

Think about drawing. Most of us drew plenty of pictures when we were children, but at a young age, we stopped. Which is why, in adulthood, most of us can't draw much better than an eight-year-old. And most of us have built lives for ourselves that don't require strong drawing abilities, so it doesn't matter. But some children have a natural aptitude for drawing and continue drawing every day, gaining confidence and skill in their work along the way. Many of those children will have parents who are also good at drawing as well, parents who encourage their children's work, offer helpful critiques, and show them that drawing is a useful skill.

In the same way, if parents aren't open-minded, don't trust each other, have poor communication skills, lack intimacy with one another, and lack proper conflict resolution skills, then it's unlikely that they will foster those skills in their children. The children won't have any good examples to model their own behavior after. And when the children begin to act close-minded, untrusting, and overly aggressive, their parents won't see a problem. After all, they've built lives for themselves where these skills aren't necessary; why should they encourage their children to develop skills that they don't believe they need themselves?

However, I don't want the takeaway of this book to be "blame your parents if your relationships keep failing." As adults, we all have the ability to take stock of our own lives and learn new skills if necessary. Of course, it's sometimes difficult to see that the habits we've developed are toxic and are damaging our ability to have healthy relationships. But if every relationship you enter ends for more or less the same reason, then it's a good idea to review your own actions and consider that you're doing something wrong. Is the problem that you can never agree with another person? That you can never trust another person? That you can never feel emotionally close to another person? That you never feel as if you're really communicating with another person? That you're always arguing with another person?

. The reason that I mentioned so many single-person case examples is that the problems in our relationships don't happen only when we get together. We each carry these bad skill sets with us throughout our lives. Only when we try to form relationships do the problems become apparent, but they were always there. That's why we should try to deal with these issues before we enter into a relationship. But the fact is that many times we can't handle these issues alone.

That's why I would recommend both couples with relationship problems and individuals who are having trouble getting into healthy relationships seek out counseling. The incidents I've described are in no way unique. Thousands of psychiatrists, therapists, priests, ministers, rabbis, imams, and counselors have heard variations on all of these stories and offered good direction for people to improve themselves. Many people will first cope with a problem by working it out between themselves, not wanting to let other people see the problems that they're having. Remember, many of the people I described made great effort to appear like healthy couples. But sometimes we're too close to our own problems to clearly see what's wrong.

Once a couple or individual realizes there's a problem, they might go to friends or family members for advice. This is a wonderful first step and many times will provide exactly the supportive advice that people need. But the fact is that we can't always count on unbiased and constructive advice from friends and family members. Many of them have long observed us and our relationships, already formed their own opinions based on that limited observation, and are all too willing to tell us who's right and who's wrong. Like ourselves, sometimes friends and family members are also too close to our problems to offer truly helpful advice.

Professional counselors, on the other hand, will provide an outsider's perspective to our problems that can be truly illuminating. Not only that, but they've also handled many other relationship problems over the years, so they have a breadth of experience that most friends and family members lack. When a couple goes to see a counselor, the counselor is far less likely to be sympathetic to one person over the other before hearing the whole story, which tends to happen when speaking with friends or family members.

Another option to consider is a support group. One of the reasons that so many people refuse to seek counseling is that they believe their problems are unique, that there's something wrong with them specifically and that nobody else will understand or be able to help. Support groups dispel that idea by placing the individual (or couple) in a room with other people dealing with the same problems. Not only that, but it's sometimes easier for us to see the problems that other people are having, offer good advice, then realize afterward that the advice would be just as appropriate for ourselves.

Most important, we must all remember that no relationship is perfect. We can't enter into relationships expecting perfection or stay out of relationships until the perfect one happens. Relationships provide us with the love and support that we need to become better people, but they also require consistent maintenance to remain strong. Only when we realize that no relationship is perfect can we truly begin the work of making our relationships stronger.

About the Author

Ira L. Lake, Ph.D., M.Div., M.A. is a Nationally Board Certified Pastoral Counselor by the Board of Christian Professional and Pastoral Counselors (BCPPC), a Cognitive Behavioral Therapy (CBT) practitioner, is a member of the Association of Christian Therapists (ACT), the National Council on Family Relations. Additionally, he is also a member of the American Association of Pastoral Counselors (AAPC).

Pastoral Counselors are clergy, Inman's, Rabbi's, and others who have received graduate education and training in both Theology and Behavioral Sciences for a clinical counseling practice that integrates both disciplines.

Dr. Lake is the President and CEO of Imtasik Family Counseling Services Inc., where clients receive integrated quality counseling and spiritual care to assist in growth and healing. Imtasik Counseling is committed to ensuring nurturance, an empathetic presence, and a safe place to transform. A belief in religion is not required to obtain counseling there; a client and his or her therapist set appropriate goals for treatment whether or not it includes a religious focus.

Dr. Lake is certified in family court mediation, chaplaincy, and grief and bereavement counseling. He has over 20 years' experience as an ordained pastor serving congregations throughout the Orange, Riverside, and Los Angeles counties, working with individuals, families, and couples in pastoral care and counseling.

Dr. Lake has completed an intensive training program for counselors with the Southern California Counseling Center and earned a doctoral degree in Human Services with a specialization in Family Studies and Intervention Strategies.

Dr. Lake is a published author with a book on Amazon called: Messed Up and Don't Even Know It: The Journey From Childhood Trauma To Healing. He is one of the nation's leading experts in Traumatic Childhood Recovery (TCR), helping survivors trace back the narratives of childhood trauma, identifying the survival mechanisms that have sabotage their chances for healthy adult relationships, and build new skills to finally grow past the abuse they suffered.

Dr. Lake specializes in couples, childhood trauma, grief and bereavement, and individual counseling. He also does workshops/seminars focusing on building and enhancing relationships. Additionally, he conducts workshops for men and women groups.